There is to be NO writing or drawing at all on this page, please. -EI

I agree. - TJ

What? Can't I even write this? How about a drawing? - TG

This page to be left blank.

I don't like this blank page at all.

This is the best PAGE in the book. - JC

Surely there should be something here? - MP

Editor: Eric Idle

Art Editor: Steve Kirwan

Artwork by Terry Gilliam

Copyright © 2009 Python (Monty) Pictures, ltd.

Photographs copyright © 2009 Python (Monty) Pictures, ltd.

Anything Goes (from "Anything Goes")
Words and Music by COLE PORTER
© 1934 (Renewed) WB MUSIC CORP.
All Rights Reserved. Used by Permission of ALFRED PUBLISHING CO., INC.

Library of Congress Cataloging-in-Publication Data

Chapman, Graham.
Monty Python live! / Graham Chapman, John Cleese, Terry Gilliam,
Eric Idle, Terry Jones, Michael Palin.
p. cm.
ISBN 978-1-4013-2367-7
1. Monty Python (Comedy troupe) I. Title.
PN2599.5.T54C47 2009
792.702'8092241—dc22
2009021541

Hyperion books are available for special promotions and premiums.
For details contact the HarperCollins Special Markets Department in the New York office
at 212-207-7528, fax 212-207-7222, or email spsales@harpercollins.com.

First Edition

10 9 8 7 6 5 4 3 2 1

MONTY PYTHON

To the always late
Graham Chapman
(1941-1989)

In loving memory.

MONTY PYTHON LIVE!

Graham Chapman

John Cleese

Terry Gilliam

Eric Idle

Terry Jones

Michael Palin

with

Executive Guest Superstars

Carol Cleveland & Neil Innes

HYPERION
•••••
New York

Foreplay

by Eric Idle

I was surprised and a little aroused recently to witness an evening of Monty Python performed entirely by women. All of them had finer breasts than us, and they were very funny, but what struck me was how well the material stood up. That was the genesis of this book. Editing it has enabled me to recall many happy hours, on stage and off, spent in the company of these cracked comrades, this small band of bickering brothers who have made me laugh longer and louder than anyone in the world.

How long ago it all seems. Who *would* have thought forty years ago we'd all be sitting here drinking Château de Chasselay? And yet forty years on, twenty-five years since we actually did anything together, interest in Monty Python is greater than ever. It's humbling. We had no idea. This book is about what greeted us when we left the sealed world of the BBC and ventured onto the broad stage of live performing. Suddenly we came face to face with a phenomenon: the monster power of television and its extraordinary ability to popularize. By chance our show was born at the dawn of the digital age, an era that is still with us. All those people who came to see us already knew all about us. Television had connected the dots.

If Graham comes across as the naughtiest boy in the school, it's only because he was the most honest. All of the boys had reason to be modest about their personal behavior at some stage of some tour. Our promoter says there were no groupies. No groupies for the promoter perhaps, but the Canadian girls were particularly friendly and there were certainly little smiles on the faces of certain boys at breakfast at various ports of call. He also claims that no hotel rooms were wrecked, so I shall draw a torn curtain over the events in Leeds. Blackmail is a dirty word. But handy. Certainly paid professionals were involved in one minor incident of hotel room wrecking, and an element of drug taking, humble by seventies standards, did take place, including the inhalation of certain substances on the balcony of a British Embassy. But I shall say no more. The publishers are paying insufficiently for such graphic details, and though the tempo of the age is to trumpet indiscretion, I believe our generation belongs in the Church of Latter Day Alzheimer's – we forget more than we forgive.

I shall not forget the many kindnesses shown by all those we encountered on our journey. John comes in occasionally for a small amount of flak for his behavior but nothing he would be ashamed of – he was always the most serious, as he was always the most hilarious. As for Graham's antics – I have left them uncensored, partly because he was proud of them, but mainly because he is dead and cannot answer back. Also he cleaned up and became virtually saintly and so is an example to others: Redemption being the current Oprahtic theme.

What follows is a collection of pictures and reminiscences from our live stage appearances, with anecdotes from the survivors plus the sketches used on these occasions. We would like to thank all those who came along with us, or were exploited, impregnated or plain disappointed by our long since vanished younger selves, and particularly Carol Cleveland and Neil Innes, to whom we are eternally insufficiently grateful.

1

Pythons
on the
Road

An Oral History…

Origins

ERIC   Performing live was my idea, I'm afraid. I had been making occasional appearances on a late night TV show called *Up Sunday!* and one week we filmed an episode from an Arts Festival in Coventry which gave me the idea. Here a screaming college audience responding loudly to only modestly funny comedy; Monty Python in this setting would absolutely kill…

The rest of the Pythons seemed vaguely amused by the idea. We had all come from college performing backgrounds; even Cheerleader Gilliam with his hand up the pants of California co-eds had performed live in public. They all agreed it would be fun, and I acted as a sort of director-producer, coordinating the gigs with the organizers, assembling lists of sketches suitable to perform live on stage, and pasting together a flimsy script. We rehearsed for a few days and then set off for Coventry. The set was non-existent but we took lots and lots of silly costumes.

1971
The Lanchester Arts Festival, Coventry
Three Midnight shows at the Coventry Arts Theater

That first evening at Warwick University was a total smash, helped no doubt by the fact that we went on after midnight. The audience were loud and raucous and drunk as skunks. We had peaked at just the right moment. We were comedy gods to these kids who had never seen us live. The laughter was loud and long and the applause deafening.

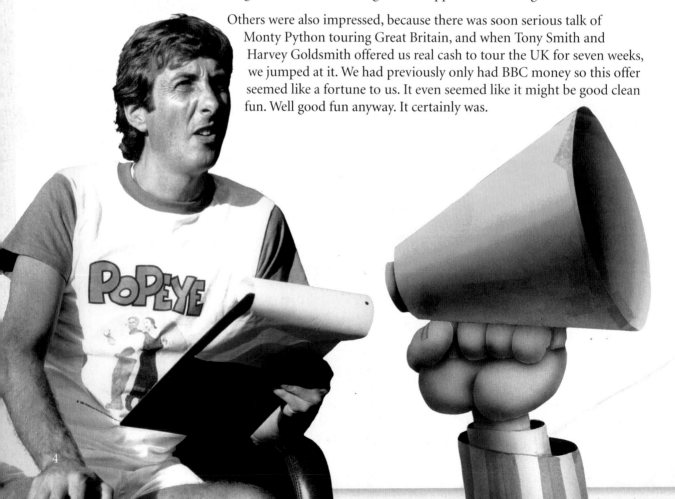

Others were also impressed, because there was soon serious talk of Monty Python touring Great Britain, and when Tony Smith and Harvey Goldsmith offered us real cash to tour the UK for seven weeks, we jumped at it. We had previously only had BBC money so this offer seemed like a fortune to us. It even seemed like it might be good clean fun. Well good fun anyway. It certainly was.

4

Graham Chapman, John Cleese, Eric Idle, Terry Jones, Terry Gilliam, Michael Palin all contributed to this oral history. The talented Carol Cleveland and Neil Innes also chimed in, and we even let our promoter, Tony Smith, our US manager, Nancy Lewis, our biographer, Kim Howard Johnson, and Carl Reiner squeeze a word in here or there.

UK Tour

April-May 24, 1973
Monty Python's First Farewell Tour
A three-week tour of the UK, 30 shows in 13 different cities

JOHN   We went round Britain in 1973, which was kind of crazy, but fun.

ERIC   We played Brighton, Bristol, Southampton, Liverpool, Manchester, Glasgow, Edinburgh, Sunderland, Norwich…

TONY SMITH   We did a whole tour around the UK, mainly in theatres, and it was fantastically successful. Chaotic, because you know, there had obviously been the Cambridge review time, they'd done it then, but since moving on to TV, they'd never really worked out how to do this in a live situation and there were quite a few problems they had to overcome.

TERRY J   It was chaotic because the sound engineer was very interested in horticulture and what happened to the brain when certain examples of it were ignited and the smoke inhaled. Since we all had individual radio microphones, it was important to keep an eye on who was on stage at any particular time and who was not, and this is not the sort of exercise that comes easily to students of horticulture. The result was that half the time on stage the audience couldn't hear us and the other half the auditorium was filled with the sound of us cursing the dope-head sound engineer in our dressing rooms.

ERIC   Our tour advanced up the left-hand coastline of England in an old black Daimler while the Bowie tour (*Aladdin Sane*) advanced up the right in several large buses. The two tours met in Glasgow, the apex, and then began to descend on opposite coasts. Bowie was carrot-haired at the time and had a brand spanking new motor home parked impressively outside our hotel. His band would troop down to breakfast in exotic glam rock drapery, white-faced and already in full make-up. This amused us no end, since we never even wore make-up on stage. Only Terry Gilliam went to see their show. The rest of us affected disinterest. We were an alternative rock-and-roll tour and we drew largely the same crowds from the universities and art schools and technical colleges. They flocked to see us. I sat opposite Harvey Goldsmith on the train south with my eyes popping as he counted the take, real money, bundles of cash, bulging in a silver metal case. There were thousands in there…

TONY   In TV you can cut to the next scene. How do you do that, how do you coordinate that and what sort of continuity can you have on a live show? You can't really say, well that was very silly and cut to something else. You've got to find a way of doing that.

Right stop that! Stop that! It's filthy! You're not even a proper woman!

Don't you oppress me, mate!

Get off! Right, where's the chap for the next skit? Hurry up.
You sit there. And…cue…the…skit!

ERIC   Graham suffered agonies of nerves about performing live. Not that we knew it but he was well on his way to becoming a fully qualified alcoholic. He had begun forgetting his words during BBC tapings and would drink to calm himself down, which of course only helped him forget them more easily. Backstage with his personal dresser and a bottle of vodka hidden in a brown paper bag he took clandestine swigs from throughout the evening.

MICHAEL   **Graham drank heavily in those days and was using the booze to cope with the extra stress and strain of the tour. This was, of course, hopeless. It is clearly possible to bang drums, run your fingers along a keyboard, or even play legendary guitar solos while unable to walk along a white line, but I've rarely seen anyone's comedy timing improved by the bottle. Graham would often come on stage late or leave the stage early, leaving the other actors to improvise as best they could.**

TONY   They, none of them really knew what they were getting into and, and neither did I.
We were all making it up as we went along.

MICHAEL   **One memorable night, in Cardiff, Graham forgot to come on at all. I was sitting on stage as Ken Shabby, a cheerfully revolting character whose job it was to clean out public toilets.**

"Is there promotion involved?" "Oh yeah! After five years they give me a brush."

Beside me on the sofa was Carol Cleveland, for whose hand in marriage I was waiting to ask her very English upper-crust father.

The sketch could not begin without Graham as the father, for he had the opening line. All I could do was paw Carol, clear my throat disgustingly, and gob on the carpet as we awaited

his arrival. After about one-and-a-half minutes of this there was still no sign of Graham, and John Cleese, waiting in the wings dressed as a bishop for the next sketch, came on in desperation and did Graham's lines, as best he could. We were all furious with Graham but the sketch never went as well again.

ERIC   Graham began to appear very late on stage. A sketch called "Ken Shabby" featured Michael as a filthy lavatory cleaner who wished to marry an innocent heiress. Graham played her father but night after night he would be absent for the start of the sketch. He had a quick change into a colonel's uniform, and young men were there to assist him and refresh him in a private booth in the wings. Each night the quick change got longer, and Michael Palin and Carol Cleveland would be left on stage helplessly awaiting his arrival. One night, hearing the silence from the audience, I stepped on to lend a hand, only to find that John was doing the same thing from the other wing. Quickly I stepped behind him and we both acted Graham's role in tandem, cracking up Michael and the audience. Finally Graham arrived and began blustering his way from the beginning again, so John and I exited in step, earning a huge round of applause. Afterwards Graham was furious and berated me (not John of course) for going on in his role. But I noticed he wasn't late again.

NEIL   It soon became apparent to the rest of us that a bizarre competition was developing between Graham Chapman and Terry Jones as to who could outdo the other with the silliest lipstick. The elderly ladies who talked in shrill voices about Jean-Paul Sartre and philosophized about shopping were known to us all as Pepperpots, from their alleged similarity of shape to a Pepper pot. For their nightly "Pepperpot" sketch

Graham and Terry each did their own make-up in opposite wings and entered the stage from opposite sides. These simple stage directions guaranteed complete surprise for both performers and onlookers alike.

It began with a frivolous "Cupid bow" from Graham causing Terry to get the giggles. Given that the sole purpose of the entire tour seemed to be degenerating into getting one's fellow performers to "corpse," this meant War! Terry responded with a bold gash of scarlet. Graham saw him and raised. He came out looking like Bozo the Clown. Terry retaliated with a large lipsticked moustache. Word spread and each night, casually at first, anyone not involved in "The Pepperpots" would gather in the wings to witness the very first "Charm Offensive."

It couldn't last. Somehow we all knew when the Final was to take place. Stage hands, technicians, dressers, half-dressed Pythons, and partisan supporters assembled on both sides of the stage eagerly awaiting their champions. Terry and his camp were looking very confident. He had covered his entire lower face with lipstick, like a scarlet Homer Simpson beard. Graham, however, clearly won because Terry cracked up when he saw him emerge. Graham had drawn a single line of lipstick from the middle of his forehead, down the side of his face, across his chin and back up to the middle of his forehead; he was wearing a complete lipstick circle!

From then on we all had to make do with Michael's brave attempts to ignore John's increasingly eccentric performances in the "Parrot" sketch.

TERRY J I *do* remember the lipstick competition. Graham started the Great Lipstick Tournament. We were both in drag and one day he came on with his lipstick smeared in a big splodge. Caught me out good and proper. The next evening I exaggerated mine and then it all spiralled out of control. The important thing was not to catch a glimpse of each other before we got on stage.

MICHAEL **I celebrated my thirtieth birthday on stage with the Pythons at the Hippodrome in Birmingham. At the end of the "Dead Parrot" sketch, John and I used to go into the "D'you want to come back to my place?" quickie. That night, instead of the usual final line of John's, "Yeah, all right," he said "No."**

I should have realised then that something was up. What happened was that the whole audience sang "Happy Birthday" as Eric's mum arrived on the stage with a birthday cake for me. As Norah Idle looked uncannily like Mary Whitehouse, a clean-up TV campaigner who hated Python, this added a further surreal touch to the evening. What could I do but go with the flow? I reprised "Gumby Flower Arranging," ending up by plunging my chrysanthemums into the cake. It was the most unforgettable birthday of my life and one of the best times on stage with the Pythons.

ERIC   Mary Whitehouse was a notorious whiner about TV morality, one of the self-appointed watchdogs who constantly complained to the BBC about standards of decency. She of course hated Monty Python. She also bore an uncanny physical resemblance to my mum. One night in Birmingham on Michael Palin's birthday we decided to surprise him with a cake. At the end of the "Parrot" sketch, John grabbed Michael while I came on as a TV announcer in a glittering dinner jacket and then brought on my mum with a birthday cake, introducing her as Mary Whitehouse. The audience gasped, convinced it was her. Michael graciously accepted the cake. He then thanked "the great shit herself for coming along," which further stunned the audience, blew out the candles, and plunged his flowers into the cake. Next day it was reported in the Birmingham paper that Mary Whitehouse had attended the Python show.

NEIL   The thing was, everyone believed the actual Mrs. Whitehouse had actually come to a Monty Python show to actually wish Michael "Happy Birthday." Such was the uncanny resemblance. I'll never forget the shocked gasp of the audience when Michael, dressed as a Gumby, took the flowers from Eric's mum and stuffed them in the cake.

TONY   It was actually very refreshing. I didn't have to get any hotel rooms repaired. I had one or two libraries we had to redecorate, but other than that it was great. No groupies.

ERIC   At Edinburgh Neil Innes and I spent the day playing miniature golf accompanied by a large bottle of malt whiskey, occasionally sitting down in a mini bunker to philosophize and sing rude songs. By night time we were so pissed we barely remembered we had a show to do and swanned in spectacularly late. Convinced we were hilarious and speaking very very slowly so the audience would get it, we personally added twenty minutes to the show. Something I vowed I would never repeat…

NEIL   Eric is wrong. We weren't drunk. We were just convinced that everything we did was that much better for being a bit slower.

TONY   We did the UK tour and it was very successful. We then said, Okay, this really does work.

ERIC   Almost before we arrived back in London people wanted more. This time we were asked to tour Canada. Summer in Canada seemed exotic, nobody except John had ventured very far in North America, and the money was very tempting.

TONY   During the course of the tour they started to talk about the fact that they were getting recognition outside of the UK. More importantly they were on CBC, Canadian broadcasting. And they said to me, you know, we're getting really popular in Canada, it would be quite nice to take this over there and do this over there. And so, I guess you know, when you're in your twenties and you've got no real barriers, you say, Well I'll do that. No problem. I'll do that.

Canada

Summer 1973
Monty Python's First Farewell Tour of Canada
A tour of Canada from Toronto to Vancouver

ERIC   The Canadian tour was pure rock and roll.

TERRY G   *I remember the flight to Canada, first class! A lounge behind the cockpit where you could drink and have a party, we were in love with being rock stars.*

ERIC   Halfway across the Atlantic Terry Gilliam was peering out of the window and someone asked him what he could see and Terry, who is after all American, said, "All I can see is a whole bunch of water." And John pilloried him mercilessly for that expression.

TERRY G   *Big bunch of water – yeah. Graham said, "He can't speak the language."*

ERIC   The flight turned into a great party and I think we'd been drinking for about six or seven hours and we came off the plane and we got through customs and there was this crowd and they went aaaargh! and screamed and we all looked behind to see if there was a rock group coming off and then we realised that they were there for us, they were there to meet us and there were all these Python fanatics and it was really strange.

TONY   We arrived at Toronto airport and there were fans there. And it was quite extraordinary. I mean it was strange, you know. None of them, as I say, none of them had been to Canada before. And there were this real crowd there was this huge enthusiasm, I mean it was a much bigger cult than we thought out there.

ERIC	It was the first time we'd had any sort of rock-and-roll kind of recognition type stuff and they put us on top of an open bus and drove us into Toronto. It was really weird, followed by cars hooting and flashing, and Canada was a bit like that, crazy, out of control.
TERRY J	It was an open-top double, and I have vague memories of hanging upside-down on the outside of the bus for a few miles. I can remember thinking, Ah this is the only way to travel…, before Neil pulled me back on board and gave me another sobering slug of whisky.
JOHN	I liked Canada. I still do. If they'd move it two thousand miles further south, I'd go live there.
CAROL	We arrived at the airport and we were really pretty silly on the plane to begin with, getting ourselves in the mood, you know, but we arrived there and we were met in the lounge by a little group of people who obviously wanted us to be very silly so we thought what can we do? And I remember Terry Gilliam and myself getting onto the luggage roundabout and I've got a photograph somewhere of us going around on this carousel.
TONY	Terry, Michael, and Eric decided that they would arrive as luggage on the luggage turntable. And there they were, rotating around the carousel. I don't think John was particularly pleased with that. He's very serious John.
CAROL	John didn't really like all that silliness.
MICHAEL	**I can remember a lot of very outrageous behaviour. Terry G particularly was on very wild form, god he just was falling about. And I remember on the carousel at the airport, he was lying on the carousel, going round and round…**
TERRY G	*I remember landing in Toronto, and there were screaming fans, not millions, thousands or hundreds, but the fact that they were aware of us was intriguing, that Python passion. We did start behaving badly like rock stars, like riding the carousel, wasn't that witty!*
	I think John was shocked by our behaviour, he didn't want to be a rock star.
ERIC	The Canadians went bonkers and I think that's what John disliked. He disliked all the rock-and-roll stuff. He didn't like it at all. He would get very annoyed when he'd come on stage and they'd laugh and applaud and he'd say "I haven't said anything funny yet!" He'd get very testy with them.
CAROL	John was not a happy chappy during that tour, which made him a little unsociable at times. He and Connie, their marriage was going through a bad time and obviously he was affected by this, so he wasn't his usual friendly self and didn't often want to go out and about with the rest of us. And there's one evening I remember very well: After the show we thought, Well let's go and eat; John had already disappeared, so a group of us went to this restaurant, and as we were paying our bill, we noticed John right over in the other end of the restaurant in a corner getting up. He'd been there all the time. So we quickly paid our bill and we thought, Let's go and follow John, and having had a copious amount of wine and feeling rather silly, we thought, We'll creep up on John and we'll jump on him from behind. Good wheeze. So we're tiptoeing along and he

suddenly stopped and we jumped into a doorway. And then he walked on further and we tiptoed closer and then he stopped and we jumped into a doorway. And we finally got very close, we were just about to pounce, and he turned around and pulled himself up to his great height and looked at us with the fiercest expression I've ever seen and then, in no uncertain terms, told us where we could go. And I remember we were all standing there going, Ooooh, we've made John angry, oh dear. So yes, it wasn't an easy time with John, that tour.

MICHAEL **People behaved quite badly on that tour, but it was just wackiness, we were sort of lads away from home and they wanted us to lark about and all that.**

So John was pretty uncomfortable with it, and you know I was a little uncomfortable with it, but I would have a drink with them and then you'd do anything…

TERRY G *We were shameless, especially Michael, Terry, and I on TV; we behaved as badly as we could because it was fun destroying the dignity of these bland shows, and to discover that the presenters were full of mischief too, anything to shock, to break down structure; we were deconstructive.*

TERRY J The trouble with TV appearances then was that we – or at least Terry G and I – felt that we had to do something to justify our time on television. Python constantly presented viewers with things they'd never seen before, and Terry and I felt we had to live up to the same expectation. Of course I realize now that an interview is just an interview and it just disappears into the endless emptiness of last night's TV. But it did make us approach our interview shows with great seriousness and planning in order to do something spontaneous and stupid.

MICHAEL **I mean the Terrys were quite wonderful on TV shows, they'd fall off their chairs and they'd tie up the presenter and all that sort of thing, and, they did it with such sheer abandon it had to be admired.**

ERIC What we would do, because they'd expect us to be funny, is that we would take the prettiest girl announcer and drag her away to the back of the stage and pretend to ravish her, which is quite funny if deeply incorrect and the rest of the TV presenters would be quite amused by this. The crew would always laugh loudly. The girls themselves always loved it because suddenly the sameness and total predictability of their world was burst open. If they had a window with a picture of downtown we'd come through the window and spoil the illusion or chuck in garbage cans first.

TERRY J As I remember it the time we kidnapped the lady news anchor was the first time CBC had aired that morning show – *Good Morning Canada*.

JOHN Audiences were great, very, very enthusiastic and much more so than in London.

CAROL The whole tour was wonderful. I don't think anybody knew what to expect as far as how we were going to be received.

ERIC They were so crazy: In Winnipeg the entire front row came dressed as a caterpillar. If the curtain goes up and you see the front row dressed like that you know you're not gonna lose that show. There's no chance that one's going down.

TERRY G *The interesting thing was all the theatres we played had exactly the same plan; they built them all the same; wherever we were they were identical. It must have been the late fifties when they had a cultural burst of activity and created all these new theatres around Canada but they were all built to exactly the same plan; it's like they had one architectural drawing that they moved from province to province. We'd travel for a thousand miles and end up with the same dressing room! It was the most weird, déjà vu-ish experience.*

TERRY J Some of them weren't designed for people with weak bladders or who like to drink two pints of beer before a show. I think it was the one in Edmonton that didn't have any aisles, so you had a sea of hundred seats across. If you were in the middle and had to go you had to say "excuse me" to fifty people.

CAROL We could be as silly and outrageous as we wanted to be and I loved every minute of it! I was glad that Neil Innes was with us too, as we both sometimes felt like we were a bit of an appendage and it was good to have him to confide in. Of course, we argued non-stop about which one of us could lay claim to being called "the seventh Python"! (It's ME Neil...it's ME!)

ERIC We were asked to do a TV show in Toronto and I think what they thought was we did improv. They said, Come in, we're gonna do a promotional thing, and they took us into a studio and they said, Here's a crate and here are some props and some toys and some squeaky things. Now just do your thing. And of course we'd never done any improv in our lives and we sucked. We were dreadful. We would try half-hearted things until we thought, What are we doing here? Because that really is the difference between what we did and what other people do. We were really disciplined writers. Python is a writer's commune. The writers dictated what was funny and only then did we cast it and only then did we rehearse it and learn it and so it's all about the writing for us. There's hardly an improv line in Python.

Do you want to come back to my place?

Yeah all right.

JOHN   The strangest audience I ever played to was in Ottawa, where on the opening night we did the jokes, and they didn't laugh. So we'd start doing the next joke and *then* they'd laugh. And we'd have to stop and wait, and then go back and start the second joke.

So I said to one of the stage hands, "What is it with this audience?"

And he said "Oh they're all politicians, they're checking to see if everyone else is gonna laugh first!"

TERRY G   *The surprise was that there were so many fans, the shows were selling out, they'd know all the material.*

TONY   I went over to Canada and rather than go the, the normal standard route where one would find an agent or a promoter for a whole tour, I went over there and did it the same way as I had in England. I went to each hall, rented the hall myself, found some publicity people in that town, in Montreal or wherever it was, and put the whole thing together. Just as if I was promoting in England. I didn't know any other way to do it, frankly. And unbeknownst to me, I was completely breaking all the rules.

NEIL   The tour of Canada was a "dartboard tour" in that it criss-crossed every time zone from east to west and back again in no particular order.

TONY   I'd really just looked at the map and sort of chosen my cities. And in terms of market research there was very little, to be honest with you. It just seemed like a good place to be.

NEIL   On the plus side however, a deal had been struck with Air Canada that allowed us all to fly first class. Basically, this meant we were entitled to free drinks.

JOHN	The Canadian tour was fun until we got way west and there was one town we hadn't sold a ticket, and someone had discovered that the television show had never gone out in that town, but had been sort of left out of the network.
TERRY J	I think it was Saskatoon. We evidently arrived at the airport but were told to carry on to Regina, where they had heard of us, and there was an empty theatre ready to take an impromptu show.
TONY	I'd never been there before in my life. So I went over there and of course it was really the blind leading the blind. But you know, you can be very convincing. You know, This way. Follow me. This is what we're doing. And they did.
MICHAEL	**I don't think any of us realised, certainly the person who planned the tour didn't realise, quite how big Canada is. So you're one night in Winnipeg, one night in Edmonton, and you know, they're thousands of miles apart. And also there was a problem because there was a go slow with the airline, and very often cargo arrived late. So you know the dead parrot would arrive a day after we needed it in some of these remote places, so you'd have to go and try and buy a dead parrot in Calgary at five in the afternoon.**
NEIL	One morning we took off from Calgary, home of the famous Stampede and the lesser-known "Tallest Tower of Its Kind in the World" - at 8:30 A.M. The "No Smoking" and "Seatbelt" signs had barely been extinguished when my early morning reverie was interrupted by an elegant air hostess.

"Would you care for a drink sir?"

"It's a bit early isn't it?" I protested, somewhat startled.

"It's eleven-thirty in Winnipeg," came the sophisticated reply.

Under her winning smile, my dithering rapidly evaporated.

"Oh all right, I'll have a gin and tonic…"

The flight droned on, and after about an hour or so, I was still nursing a good third of what had been a very liberal helping of the popular Happy Hour beverage when the captain's deep, soothing voice was suddenly heard throughout the aircraft.

"Would passenger Thompson kindly make himself known to the cabin crew."

For some strange reason, a scene from the movie *Spartacus* flashed across my mind. I stood up and boldly declared, "I'm passenger Thompson!"

I dare say it would have fallen quite flat had not Graham Chapman had precisely the same thought at precisely the same time and leapt to his feet:

"I'm passenger Thompson!"

And then everyone else was up, joyously re-enacting the famous scene with uncanny aplomb.

"I'm passenger Thompson!"

"I'm passenger Thompson!"

I'm sure Air Canada was really glad to see the back of us.

ERIC   At the time Air Canada was having a strike, but it was a very Canadian strike. They didn't stop work, they just slowed down a bit. The only thing affected was our set. It was always a day or two behind us. We would be in Edmonton and hear rumors it had arrived in Winnipeg. Moose Jaw, though the gig was cancelled, did receive a visit from our set. In fact we never actually saw our legendary set, comfortably beating it to the end of the tour in Vancouver. Fortunately we had our film footage: "Silly Olympics," "Philosophers' Football," and "Buzz Aldrin in a Fairy Tale," which we had shot in Germany for two German TV specials, and which was priceless for us as it was new Python to the audience. Mercifully we also had our costumes, so all we needed was a screen and a few chairs. In fact I still don't know what the set looked like. It's probably still touring Canada…

TONY   And so, it turned out very well because I think we sold out, even in places like French Canada, we weren't quite sure how that was going to be, they didn't quite get it all I don't think. But even in Montreal it was really good. I mean great audiences and I don't think any of us made a fortune out of it. I have to say that. I think that we probably all came out with about five hundred dollars each at the end of the day. But it was great fun. I mean it was, it was just good fun.

ERIC   So the Canadians used it as a great festival and they always said, "Oh we always get stoned and watch the TV Show. You must be so stoned to write it." And we said, "What do you mean stoned? You're kidding. No way. We work nine to five. You can't write if you're stoned. You'll never find the typewriter."

TONY   Bookings were pretty good. Even in places as obscure as Saskatoon.

MICHAEL   **We were in Regina, and Regina's just in the middle of open plains of cornfield, mile after mile, nothing but flat plains. And I remember Graham looking at it, in that little way he used to, in a slightly reflective way. And the man said, "So this is Regina, what do you think?" And Graham said, "Oh why didn't they put it over there?"**

TONY   Graham had this book *A Gay Guide to Canada*. And the one place it didn't have any entry was Regina. And Regina is the headquarters of the Canadian Royal Mounted Police. That's where they do all their training. So it was Graham's mission to pull a Mountie. And he did. In Regina. I have no idea how, but, yes, he came back quite triumphant.

GRAHAM   Thirty-five thousand feet up in the air with an Eskimo in the toilet of a Boeing 747…

NANCY LEWIS   *I was staggered at Graham Chapman's genuine lunacy. I remember going to his room in Canada, and there were salad plates with salad all around his room and I said, "What is this?" and he had found out that on Sundays in Canada even in a hotel the only way you could get a drink of alcohol was to order food, and the salad was the least expensive thing on the room service menu, so he kept ordering salad so he could have another drink. There were salads all over the room.*

CAROL   In Vancouver we were immediately thrown into a large cage as soon as we arrived at the airport! We came out of the airport and there's an enormous cage set up, this colossal cage, and

16

we thought, What's that about? and they asked us to get in the cage. We couldn't understand why, very bizarre, but we complied, got in the cage, and they wanted us to be like animals, which I thought was very strange. I never quite understood why. I guess word had got out that we were somewhat wild and untamed.

ERIC   When we got to Vancouver the Promoters had created a cage for us to stand in as a photo opportunity. I remember we were all rather embarrassed about it – but fortunately Terry Jones saved the day by totally destroying it.

JOHN   I got to Vancouver, which I love, one of my favourite cities ever. And there was a heatwave in Vancouver. And when I came off stage at the end of the show on the first night there wasn't a square inch of my shirt that was not soaked with sweat, and so I towelled myself off and I was totally dehydrated. And all I could think about was a long cold beer. And I got to the stage door and opened it and there were two hundred people there.

"Oh John Cleese, John Cleese, John Cleese!"

And I said, "I'm not John, I'm his brother Colin, he's just coming."

And to my utter amazement they parted and let me walk through. And thirty seconds later I was drinking a cold beer. I could never believe I got away with that one.

ERIC   On the way to Vancouver two things happened on the plane. John announced he wasn't gonna do any more Python and that was kind of a shock and then we got an offer to go down to LA to promote the record for Buddha Records. They would fly us down to do some promotion of our albums because we were known only as a recording group in America. So we all flew down to San Francisco except for John, who went home. He always seemed to miss the fun things, because this was a real fun time. I don't think any of us had been in the States before and San Francisco was our entry into the United States.

NANCY   *I met them in San Francisco. They agreed to come down there to do some promotion for Buddha at that stage. They weren't eager, shall we say? I said well Buddha would pay the expenses of that portion of the trip, to come to San Francisco and LA, and they did. I believe John didn't come at all.*

17

Everyone else came to San Francisco. We had a photo session for Rolling Stone *I remember in the parking lot of the hotel and Annie Leibovitz took the photo. Neil was in it with his back to the camera standing in for John Cleese!*

ERIC   We stayed at a Japanese hotel with a bathroom with instructions on "How To Take A Bath" in Japanese, and little pictures like an airplane emergency brochure. I thought that was funny. Then Terry G, Nancy, and I drove down to LA along the Pacific Coast Highway, Big Sur, staying overnight in a motel. And when we got to LA they put us in the Riot House, you know, the Hyatt House on Sunset, which was filled with English rock-and-roll groups busy having a fantastic time and we just fit right in. We'd go to the Roxy and the Whiskey just down on the strip and have fun.

MICHAEL **When we went down to LA after Canada, Graham had had so much to drink, he checked into this hotel on Sunset and had to ring down to check whether he'd checked in. They told him yes he'd checked in. Well, he said, in that case he wanted to go to a restaurant that he knew, and can he have a limousine? And they said, You want a limousine? And Graham said, Yeah, yeah I want a limousine, I want to go to the restaurant. They said, are you sure you want a limousine for the restaurant? He said, Yes, you may not know who I am but I would like a limousine now thank you very much, so get the limousine ready. So Graham goes down and gets in the limousine and only at the moment did he realise that the restaurant he was talking about was just opposite the hotel; he just went across the road in the limousine and got out.**

NANCY   *Ron Weisner, who was in charge of artist relations and all the TV bookings for Buddha, was quite brilliant, and he said, "Hey we got them a slot on* The Tonight Show."

ERIC   We'd come down from Canada and we were comedy gods and they laughed at anything we did, coming out they laughed, going in they laughed, even going home, waving goodbye oh so witty. We just could not fail to get a laugh.

NANCY   *Well I was very excited, I thought,* Wow The Tonight Show, *this is fabulous, we'll get a huge market. And then we got there and realised Johnny Carson was on holiday and Joey Bishop was hosting the show.*

ERIC   So we came into LA and we were on *The Tonight Show* with Joey Bishop and he said, "Now here are some people from England, I don't know who they are, I've never heard of them but apparently they're funny."

NANCY   *Joey Bishop was a very deadpan sort of monotone type of guy. I remember clearly his introduction. He said, "Hey there are these guys from England. I hear they're supposed to be funny," and they went into sketches immediately.*

ERIC   The curtain went up and there were two of us dressed as little old ladies in grey wigs shrieking at each other.

"Have you buried the cat yet?"

"No it's not dead yet. Still coughing up blood."

And it was like that shot in *The Producers* where the audience are staring open-mouthed in disbelief. Total silence.

NANCY	*They did a "Pepperpot" sketch, and the audience sat there. Nothing went through. And my heart was sinking. I thought, This is it, you know, they will never speak to me again.*
ERIC	We had half an hours material to do and we did it in twenty minutes. We didn't get a single laugh. It was fantastic.
TERRY J	I *do* remember the Joey Bishop show vividly. Talk about being in the wrong place at the wrong time and in front of the wrong audience. Funny I can remember that but not the adulatory crowds…
NANCY	*We just thought, This is a total disaster in front of the nation on a big major television network debut, and there it was. Dead. It was terrible.*
ERIC	And it was such a high we raced outside and we laughed and we laughed and we rolled around on the ground laughing because it was so funny: Here we'd been doing this stuff to standing ovations all over Canada and we come here to standing silence and it was just really funny, it was truly one of the funniest things I remember about Python.
NANCY	*Thank heavens they did. Wasn't that wonderful? I mean they were as a group the least ambitious for American success. They did not come here saying, "Oh we gotta make it in America." Because if they had, if they had cared at all, they would have been ready to pack it in after* The Tonight Show.
ERIC	For some reason we were booked on *The Midnight Special*, a kind of rock-and-roll show, and Terry and I did "Nudge Nudge" and I don't know what anybody else did.
TERRY J	It was kind of a music show, there were some bands in the studio, and Neil Innes was there, on stilts like a very tall guitar player.
NANCY	*We also had got them onto* The Midnight Special. *We taped some excerpts that were used. They did a Gumby sketch, I can't remember what else.*
ERIC	I just remember doing "Nudge Nudge" with Terry in a bowler hat and it went over very well with the kids, they got it at once and I think the sketch then played every week for about fifteen or sixteen years, because that's how America knows "Nudge." It was one of the sketches that they became really familiar with.
NANCY	*George Schlatter invited us over to Jerry Weintraub's house and Jerry was saying to me, "These guys have to make a movie. Come on, I'll finance it."*

And I said, "Fine, I just don't think they're keen to at the moment."

And Jerry said, "I'll give them a million dollars. I'll write out a cheque today."

I said, "Fine, why don't you go tell them that?" because Eric and Michael were playing badminton in the backyard. And he went out there and they never interrupted their game and Jerry said, "I'll give you a million bucks" and that was a lot of money in those days. And they said, "No, we're not interested," and just went on with their game.

And he came back and he said, "You're right, they really aren't."

KISS ME!

London

March 1974

Monty Python Live at Drury Lane!
A two-week run, extended to four, at London's Theatre Royal, Drury Lane

MICHAEL **At a Python meeting we decide to call our Drury Lane show *Monty Python's First Farewell Tour (Repeat)* and overprint it with the words "NOT CANCELLED."**

ERIC Oddly there seem to be very few reminiscences about the London run, probably for the simple reason that we were not on the road. We all came from our separate homes and returned to them. I remember that my current wife, Lynn Ashley, was in the show and that we had a one-year-old baby in our dressing room. I remember the crowds were raucous and star-studded – the Stones came, Pink Floyd, various Beatles, all of London café society – but we all returned to our homes and no one is a hero to his wife…

TERRY J Yes, the Drury Lane run was the nearest most of us ever got to having a proper job. Saying goodbye to the wife. Going out to work (night shift) and returning home later that night drunk as skunks.

MICHAEL **At the Theatre Royal, Drury Lane, for a press party to launch our two-week "season," I see Monty Python is not over-announced on the outside. At least we have our name on paper, if not in lights. Inside, there is a box office without a queue. Up the wide staircase to the Circle Bar, which is of the proportions of Adam's library at Kenwood House, with four huge Corinthian columns dwarfing a motley collection of about thirty press folk.**

Nicholas de Jongh of *The Guardian*, looking tubby and rather windswept, moved amongst us with an uncertain, rather indulgent smile and a notebook, asking us for witty things to say.

At least Eric had something reasonable (which appeared next morning in the paper). He was feeding his son Carey at the time, and replied, "It was all right for Oscar Wilde, being gay. He didn't have to feed babies, he had both arms free for being witty."

N de J: "But Oscar Wilde had children."

El: "Trust *The Guardian* to know that."

NEIL The Pythons were initially supposed to be doing two weeks live at Drury Lane, but such was the demand for tickets we ended up doing four.

MICHAEL The approach to the auditorium, the passageways and halls, are furnished and decorated in the grand classical style. Doric columns, porticoes, domes, balustrades, and statues of great actors in niches. On the walls flanking the wide and impressive staircases are huge oil paintings. It somehow feels as likely and as suitable a venue for Python as a power station. The size of the auditorium would a year ago have made me laugh and run out straightaway to return Tony's contract, but having rehearsed in the Rainbow, and played the Wilfred Pelletier Theatre in Montreal, both of which hold over 3,000 seats, the wide open spaces of the Theatre Royal (2,200 seats) no longer hold quite the same terror. Nevertheless, the sight of three balconies and innumerable lavishly decorated boxes, and a general air of London opulence and tradition, tightened my stomach a little.

TERRY J It was initially a nerve-wracking proposition, but at the same time it was somehow reassuring to find ourselves part of the "theatrical establishment" even if it was an illusion.

ERIC We put the Pantomime Princess Margaret in the Royal Box, and every night before the show started, she would come out and wave and the audience would go crazy.

NEIL 1974 was a year of two elections so it was decided that the "Election" sketch should be included. For me this meant a most uncomfortable quick change every night. I had to dash off and put on: a bowler hat (no problem), a false moustache (easy), a light coat (don't even think about it), and a pair of frogman's flippers... (What?) That's right a pair of fucking frogman's flippers. Every night I was almost in tears with the difficulty of this task. And for what? So I could enter briefly as Kevin Phillips-Bong (Silly Party) and be asked by Eric,

"Are you at all downhearted by your defeat?"

For twenty-seven days I dutifully replied: "Oh no, not at all. As I always say, try, try, try again."

However, on the last night of Drury Lane I decided to build my part into something more worthy of my stature as an Actor. To underuse someone of my talent and make them wear aquatic rubber goods was quite simply "de trop." So when Eric asked me if I was "at all down-hearted," I looked him in the eye and reached for the microphone. Fortunately he was also in the mood for some "end of term" fun and he handed it over, grinning horribly…

"Oh no, not at all, as I always say, try, try, try again…"

By now I was flapping my way to the front of stage,

"… climb every mountain, ford every stream, follow every rainbow until you find your dream."

And then I made the fateful error of launching into song.

"A dream that will last for as long as you live…"

What I had forgotten was that a mobile multi-track recording studio was outside getting all of this on tape. Anyway, it was adjudged to be "very funny" by the Pythons and included on their album *Monty Python Live at Drury Lane*. Months later, a vast amount of Python money had to be forked over to the publishers of *The Sound of Music*. Revealing the exact amount of these "royalties" I leave to the discretion of the editor.

JOHN   London was puzzling to play to because on the first night we came out and did the first few lines, and there was a tremendous reception as if we'd scored the winning goal of the Cup Final. Whoosh! Wow! Yeah! And then we would play the sketch to complete silence,

and then do the last line, and it was Whoosh! Wow! Yeah! again. And I was very puzzled and I came off and said to a stagehand, "What is going on here? They're not laughing."

And he said, "Come and look," and he took me to the curtain, and part of the curtain's got this tiny piece of gauze so you can look out and see the audience. And I looked, and somebody else was on stage doing a sketch and the audience were looking intently and mouthing the words. They were doing the lines to themselves along with the performers.

"You have to see" he said, "this is not a show, this is like a rock concert, they know the songs, they know the sketches, they're just coming to celebrate being with you."

MICHAEL **The reviews have been surprisingly extensive – it takes a second-hand collection of old TV material for critics to start taking Python really seriously. Harold Hobson was greatly impressed and called us true Popular Theatre – and Milton Shulman, perhaps our first critical friend on the TV series, was equally enthusiastic. Despite the fact that it's an old show, already touted in the provinces and Canada, London critics have devoted enormous space to analyzing it, even in the grudging *Observer* review (which described Terry and myself as "virtually indistinguishable" and tending "to screech lot").**

ERIC I remember the hardest part of the show was having to host the hundreds of people who insisted on coming backstage afterwards to your dressing room demanding free drinks and a chance to stare at you changing.

MICHAEL **We're in the fortunate position of not having to rely on reviews to sell our seats. Despite the fact that Drury Lane holds 2,200 people, we are booked solid for two weeks, we have extended our run to three weeks, and at every performance there are apparently touts out the front selling tickets for five to ten pounds.**

New York

April 14-May 2, 1976
Monty Python Live!
Four weeks of sell-out shows at City Center, New York

MICHAEL **We held a very cordial Python meeting at Park Square East to discuss the content of our stage show in New York. Once again it proved that Python works well as a group when discussing the creation of sketches and jokes – the reason, after all, why we originally got together. Today, "Blackmail" was added to the list, John having said that, although he may be sounding rather selfish, he wanted to cut down the number of sketches he appeared in, and he felt that I was very light in number of appearances. So "Michael Miles" out and "Blackmail" came in. Graham protested briefly, but the general consensus was that "Cocktail Bar" should go, along with the "Bruces" and the "Pepperpots" in a big purge of the generally accepted weak middle of the first half. In went "Salvation Fuzz" (entirely new to stage), "Crunchy Frog" (ditto) – with Graham taking John's role as Inspector Praline – and an amalgamation of various "Courtroom" sketches to replace "Silly Elections" as a closer.**

ERIC New York is named New York because it likes the new and that's what it's really good at. It picked up on us very quickly and they threw a big party in Union Square Station. We opened on Yom Kippur – whether that was deliberate or they felt no Jews would ever like Python I'm not sure.

CARL REINER *Yes, not one Jew among them. That's wonderful to know because I get that all the time, they say, Why are all the comedians Jews? And I mention the people that are not Jewish, I say Bob Hope and so on, and now I can say Monty Python. I've got a whole bunch of non-Jews.*

ERIC   We had a very good opening night and there was a huge party. I remember Leonard Bernstein in a cape and all these famous people and Paul Simon introduced me to Chevy Chase and Lorne Michaels who took me back to meet John Belushi, and then I think the next night I went to see *Saturday Night Live*, with Terry Gilliam after our show, and it was their first season and they had a puppet sketch – and we thought, Well this is a bit uncool, you know, puppets on your fucking show. Then they went off to England and became *The Muppet Show*!

TERRY J   We were crossing the road when this fan stopped his car in the middle of the street, leapt out, and ran up to us. He was very effusive and said how great it was to see us and that his name was Jim Henson. I think we managed to be quite polite to him, but looking back I feel terrible we didn't go: "Oh my God! Not *the* Jim Henson!"

It was the same when Nancy Lewis took us out to dinner with a Python enthusiast called Marty Scorsese. He'd just made a film called *Mean Streets* which none of us had even heard of, of course, and so the entire meal was spent with him raving on about Python. Terribly embarrassing in retrospect.

MICHAEL   **At the opening party I meet John Cale, another complete Python fan. A breathless PR lady rushes up and asks me to come and have my photo taken with Leonard Bernstein. This means being pulled through the crowds of ordinary plebs and being held in position, like a greyhound in a stall, whilst Lenny finishes talking to someone else. Then, after a while, Lenny turns, shakes my hand. He's smaller than I expected; short and dynamic. The flashbulbs go crazy. Lenny introduces me to Adolph Green, another songwriter, who is nice and quiet and amiable. As I talk to Lenny I'm actually being pulled to one side by this wretched PR lady so that I don't spoil the shot by obscuring his face from the cameras. He goes on about how he and his kids adore the show. Later he asks John and Eric to do bits of sketches and Eric replies by demanding that Bernstein sing a bit of Beethoven.**

Clearly the little fellow loves the publicity and plays up to it – sending it up rotten, but playing along nevertheless, and, always behind and around, the acolytes, the standers and watchers. It's the NY treatment, and it goes on till two or three – I forget which – when the waiting limousine whisks us back, exhausted.

TERRY G   *We were the toast of the town in New York, we were it, Andy Warhol was there, I was in a daze, all these famous people smiling at you, I don't know what to do I'm in a daze.*

TERRY J   Actually the bit of star-spotting that made the biggest impression on me was nothing to do with the Python shows. Nancy Lewis had organized a brownstone house in Turtle Gardens for Michael and me and our families. I think it had belonged to the editor of the *New Yorker,* and we were told that our next-door neighbor was none other than Katharine Hepburn!

Well one morning I was standing at the end of our garden looking back towards the houses when I realized I could see into the basement kitchen of the house next door, and there was the Great Diva herself, checking her groceries against her grocery list. That, I thought, was real life.

NANCY   *I think it was actually a shock to the Pythons when they first did City Center. It was the first time they'd done their show live in America. They were taken aback at how many people recited the sketches with them, like "Dead Parrot" and "Lumberjack."*

CAROL   My goodness, that first night was an eye-opener. I mean it was incredible because we were totally treated like pop stars. I mean here were all these people who seemed to know the sketches extremely well and they whooped and they wailed and they were dressed as Gumby's and all sorts of strange characters and we could hardly get a word out. We couldn't hear ourselves. I'd never experienced anything like that. I don't believe the guys had either and that was the first time I thought wow, yes, we made it in America. This is exciting.

NANCY   *And when it came out it was very well reviewed, and Clive Barnes, who was then the critic for the New York Times, I remember seeing him afterwards at the opening night party.*

I remember John Cleese going up to Clive Barnes having read the New York Times review, because it came out that night, and saying, "Would it be appropriate if I were to kiss you on the lips?" I mean Clive Barnes gave him a wonderful review and John wasn't sure if it was appropriate to kiss a critic of the New York Times.

27

ERIC We were very much feted at City Center. I mean they really liked us. I remember we started off and we would just go out of the stage door and there'd be two or three people and we'd sign autographs. But every night there were more. Suddenly there were ten people and then there were twenty people and then there were forty people. In the end we had to get in a limo backstage and do the full rock-and-roll exit because there were just too many people and I thought, Oh, that's interesting, how these things snowball. Then the limo would just drop us round the corner and we could walk home, nobody gave a toss who we were.

CAROL There was a wonderful moment that first night, when we came out of the stage door after the show, and there was an Ahhhhh, and the screaming fans, there were about a hundred screaming fans and Michael was the first one out and they all came rushing towards us and I remember this one girl rushed forwards, threw herself at Michael, who is the shy one, and promptly fainted in his arms and I remember him sort of standing there with this girl draped over him, not knowing what to do. After that we thought, Well we can't go out the stage door, so the next few nights we'd have to get into a limo inside the stage door, the grill would go up, and we'd shoot out and all these people would see the car and come chasing, you know, about a hundred people chasing this limo up Fifth Avenue. It was incredible.

TERRY G *It was like a pop concert, everyone mouths along. I got bored, because I didn't have much to do, and it was repetitive, but it was nice being in New York and feeling that crowd, it was packed. For all preceding nights it was jolly and we simply walked off, but on the last night the security was really high, limos had to take us out of a secure area, and the minute you do that you create a frenzy; it was absurd, it made total chaos, for a brief moment we felt like the Beatles or Rolling Stones, and someone might get hurt!*

CAROL The guys were not exactly what one could call snazzy dressers and I think it's safe to say that the two Terrys rather excelled in "Can't-be-bothered-chic." One evening we went to what was reputedly the best steak restaurant in the city, which also turned out to be the most pretentious: candelabra on the tables and waiters in black tie and tails. I dressed up and, as usual, the guys dressed down in jeans. I warranted a little smile and a carefully placed napkin, whilst the guys got a look of disdain and napkins dropped on their laps. We brought with us a bottle of champagne and were charged three times as much for corkage. Terry J inquired about the cost of a very fine burgundy. "It's rather expensive!" came the reply. Our steaks were eventually placed before us, at which stage Terry G promptly picked his up and plonked it on his head! A stunned pause and then Terry J followed suit. How I wish I'd had a camera!

MICHAEL **One of the worst times was at the end of the City Center shows in New York in 1976, when my voice, never very good after roaring out Gumby, disappeared completely. And there**

were two shows still to go. **My diary entry for that day gives an impression of the pain and the panic, but misses out one choice detail. My longest speech in the show came in the "Silly Walks" sketch when I explain to John at great length about my walk and why I want money to develop it. At the last show, with an epic straining of the vocal chords, I managed to struggle to the end of it and sat back in relief. John looked at me for a moment then shook his head, "I'm sorry. What was that again?"**

NEIL   Poor Michael was really upset whenever he lost his voice and a glum Palin can resemble a hungry dog in sight of a biscuit. So I felt a bit mean offering him a stiff malt whisky. "Will it make my voice come back?" he croaked. "No, but you won't care anymore" was clearly cold comfort, but he graciously attempted a chuckle. And managed a small refill.

TERRY J   We all did drink far too much anyway. We didn't take drugs but we drank a hell of a lot. In fact I can't remember how much we drank precisely because of the amount we drank. If I had space in my brain to remember all the pints of beer and bottles of wine we got through I'd have a brain the size of Einstein's—or at least the average whale's.

CAROL   Mind you, it wasn't all fun...Graham was mugged in a club, Neil had his apartment broken into, I too had an item nicked from my place, and John had his wallet stolen by two "ladies of the night" while innocently walking back to his hotel!

MICHAEL   **At the theatre Neil tells me that their flat has been burgled. He's now about the fourth or fifth of the Python group to have lost money or had it stolen since we arrived in NY. Charles Knode, Mollie Kirkland (the stage manager), and Carol have all had money taken and, in a strangely un-detailed episode, I gather that John C. was rolled by a couple of hookers!**

CAROL   One day, four of us set off by helicopter for Philadelphia to appear on *The Mike Douglas Show*, where we were met with total bemusement. The Black Knight clip from *The Holy Grail* left the studio audience in jaw-dropping silence! Only one thing for it...get silly. Mike Douglas's attempt at a serious interview with the guys failed completely so he turned his attention to me, saying, "Now, I'm sure I can get a straight answer out of you, Carol." At that point Terry Gilliam, who had crept up behind me unseen, grabbed hold and yanked me backwards over the sofa with my legs up in the air. The rest of the interview disintegrated into chaos and I'm happy to say there were more like that to follow.

MICHAEL   **At one show someone was letting off firecrackers very irritatingly. It came to a head in "Argument," in which a very loud crack completely obscured a line and Graham leaped in,**

29

George Harrison joins the choir.

doing his favourite bit, yelling at hecklers. As he had just done "The Man Who Gives Abuse"…it all fit very neatly. The offender was seen to be forcibly removed from the theatre by Jim Beach. Graham's volleyball of abuse followed him right up the aisle. The sketch went swimmingly after that.

ERIC We always closed with "The Lumberjack Song," which I had to sing as Michael had always lost his voice by then. One night, George Harrison came to see the show and we suggested he join us on stage as a Mountie in the chorus for the final singalong. We dressed him up in a red tunic and a Mountie hat and he went on with the others. He behaved impeccably, singing along totally inconspicuously, and absolutely no one in the audience noticed we had a Beatle on stage with us. It was a thrill for him, as his pseudonym on his last tour was Jack Lumber.

MICHAEL **At the show tonight George Harrison, looking tired and ill and with short hair, fulfils what he calls a lifetime's ambition and comes on as one of the Mountie chorus in "The Lumberjack Song." He's very modest about it, wears his hat pulled well down and refuses to appear in the curtain call. He's now off on holiday to the Virgin Islands. He needs it.**

ERIC Harry Nilsson, hearing about George's appearance, decided he'd do the same thing. Nobody objected and we dressed him up in the same costume. Unfortunately he had "had a few" so that instead of remaining incognito he refused to remove his shades, waved around on stage drunkenly, and generally alerted the audience to his presence. When the curtain came down at the end of the song, we all had to take a step backwards to let it drop. Instead of joining us, Harry stepped forward, arms outstretched to the roar of the crowd. The curtain fell. "Where's Harry?" we asked. The curtain rose again. No Harry. He had walked straight forward and fallen off the stage into the audience. How we laughed…Sadly he broke his wrist.

MICHAEL   **Harry Nilsson joins us on stage for "The Lumberjack Song." He is coked to the eyeballs and full of booze too, but grins benignly and seems to be enjoying himself, when, at the last curtain call, I see him suddenly lurch forward towards the edge of the stage, presumably to fraternize with the cheering audience. As he goes forward, the curtain starts to fall and, before we can pull him back, Harry keels over into the front row and lies helplessly astride the wooden edge of the orchestra pit. The curtain descends, leaving us with this bizarre vision of a drunken Mountie lying on top of the audience!**

NEIL   Of all the exalted guests who appeared "incognito" as a Mountie at the end of the "Lumberjack" sketch, Harry Nilsson was the most conspicuous. He was the only one whose buttons were done up incorrectly and whose hat was too jaunty. Failing to stand up again after a bow and disappearing into the orchestra pit was also a bit of a giveaway.

TERRY J   I remember Harry Nilsson coming on as a Mountie for "The Lumberjack Song." In the middle of it he lit a firework which shot across the audience's heads and exploded in the Circle Bar, creating a cascade of Golden Rain which unfortunately fell onto the end-of-show drinks that had been laid out ready. A lot of the drinks happened to be whisky and bourbon, and these ignited, causing a conflagration that quickly spread into the auditorium. There was panic as spectators scrambled over each other to get to the exits. Forty people were trampled to death and the rest were incinerated in the raging inferno that had so recently been a place of innocent mirth and amusement.

MICHAEL   **During one show a two-foot-long prick was thrown on stage during the "Bruces" sketch. Eric picked it up.**

"Oh look, Bruce," he said, "one of those little American penises."

TERRY J   We never really got any groupies. Unfortunately comedy groupies are not the kind of people you'd want to get into bed with so we didn't really get the perks that the singers get, I'm afraid.

GRAHAM   New York was "Fun City." How about that time in Raffles' Bar – good-looking Puerto-Rican?... Vrooom! – Straight into the telephone booth with him. We didn't give a damn – we were young and in love. For three whole minutes we grappled with each other, but, out of concern for the other patrons of the bar, we left the door of the booth open – if we'd closed it the lights would have gone on...

KIM HOWARD JOHNSON

My only encounter with Graham backstage at City Center was between shows on a Saturday night, and Graham was pretty well in the bag, walking around, occasionally screeching, calling "Betty Marsden" or singing "Ya De Buckety."

ERIC   That was a fun time, City Center. We had a good time. Nudge nudge.

Hollywood Bowl

September 2-29, 1980
Monty Python Live at The Hollywood Bowl!
Four nights under the stars for 8,000 fans a night.

MICHAEL   **The Hollywood Bowl was, I think, probably the best experience of all those stage performances we did, because it was just a great place, an iconic place.**

CAROL   Going to the Hollywood Bowl, I think, was the pinnacle of Python. Especially for me because I was brought up there, just outside Los Angeles, so I was going home, and all my chums from high school were gonna come and see me. Wow. It was a wonderful experience. We only did four nights but we were playing to eight, nine thousand people a night and I think there were only about ten of them who didn't know every word to every sketch.

TERRY G   *Hollywood Bowl was interesting. We got an offer to do it for $1 million for the six of us from Alan Tinkley, but Dennis O'Brien took over the project and Alan was pushed out. Dennis was after a quick Python movie and he brought the cameras in, and of course in the end we didn't get the money, we had to release the film over here, to try and get the money back, the million had somehow evaporated, and that was the beginning of the end for us and HandMade Films. He had no idea between our money and his money…*

CAROL The first time we walked out on that stage, and you know it's an open-air place so the sound of eight thousand people, all shouting out the words before we opened our mouths, and they're whooping and they're wailing and they're carrying on, it took a while to get used to it. The first night we could hardly get a word out.

CARL REINER *Well as soon as they came over I invited them to my house. Michael Palin and Eric Idle and Terry Gilliam came over and had Chinese food, and they were regular people, they spoke English, and we just talked about life and things. You can't be silly unless you know what the basic rules of life are. You can't make fun of life unless you really understand life. You can't make fun of it unless you've been there. And they were I think about to do the Hollywood Bowl and they were nervous about how they were going to go. Oh boy did they ever tear that place apart? They really tore the place apart. Whatever it was that PBS did by disseminating their sketches meant they had a raft of fans here ready for them. And we're still ready. We went to see them there at the Bowl and you know it's funny to this day I don't think I've ever laughed as much as at "The Ministry of Silly Walks."*

CAROL We did start mucking about after that first night, when we realised what sort of audience we had, we mucked about quite a bit by the end of it. I do remember, for instance, we thought, Well let's fool them because they know all the words, let's try and get one over on them. And for instance the "Travel Agent's" sketch, which involved Michael as a travel agent at his desk, me as his secretary at my desk, and Eric comes on as a man wanting to book the holiday. And the way it went in the TV show is Eric comes up to me and I'm doing my nails and I have a look at him and just say, "Oh, have you come about a holiday or would you like to come upstairs?"

So this is what the audience thinks I'm going to say, which I did on the first night. The second night, while we were in the wings, I thought, no, let's say something else. So on the second night Eric comes up to me, I look up at him and say, "Hello, have you come about a holiday, or would you like a blow job?"

Stunned silence. Eight thousand people, silence. And then you heard "what did she say?" and then whoosh, a great uproar. And we started having a lot of fun with them after that.

TERRY G *The shows were great fun, cause the crowds were huge, massive, we wouldn't go on till they were screaming, we'd ad-lib to make the others corpse, entertaining ourselves. I remember the rehearsals and then driving in and I couldn't get in, the Nazis had arrived for security, stopping me from getting into the show; we'd jumped to big-stadium level of security, immense; then afterwards there was a big tent for a green room, and all of Hollywood turned up.*

TERRY J Our audience was about eight thousand, I believe. We filled the Hollywood Bowl for four nights. But I remember feeling a bit humbled when one of the groundsmen took us back behind the line of fir trees that marked the very back of the auditorium. The trees were movable, and behind them the seating stretched out in a fan waiting for their maximum audience of thirty thousand.

CAROL The curtain calls were wonderful. I thought the curtain calls were the best part of the show actually. We started off just doing two or three and then we'd just go on doing curtain calls, making them up, doing silly stuff. The guys would say to me off stage, "Carol, run across the stage," and I'd run and they would all chase me, and then we'd turn around and they would run across and I'd chase them. And then we'd break into a cancan for the next one – whatever came into our heads.

And the audience was going crazy, they loved it, and eventually we would get bored and go off to the VIP lounge and the audience would still be there, waiting for us until finally we'd put up big signs on the screen saying "Piss Off." And they still didn't leave. We'd go home and they were still there.

CARL REINER *It was interesting because it was like a rock concert where everybody came to hear their favourite song. You know, Is Sinatra going to sing "My Way"? And so there were people there actually with total knowledge of everything they've ever done. They were mouthing things. You know it's funny when the thing is that good you want everybody to see it and you're hoping they're going to do this and that. And they did. They didn't disappoint. People were screaming. It was a triumph, a triumph. "The Ministry of Silly Walks" is still the thing to put on your list of all-time best favourites.*

JOHN   But it was very strange to go out there and one or two nights, if you forgot lines, 'cause Michael always made a point of trying to break me up, 'cause he's a very treacherous creature. And if he could ad-lib something, particularly in the "Parrot" sketch, I'd ask him for a new parrot, one that's alive, and he'd come back and say, "Well we're fresh out of parrots."

I'd say, "Well, what else have you got?"

He'd say, "I've got a slug."

I'd say, "Does it talk?"

And he's supposed to say, "Not much."

So that night he said, "Well it mutters a bit."

And I laughed, and turned upstage and by the time I got myself back under control, I couldn't remember where we were in the sketch. I'd completely gone. But I was just so relaxed I said to the audience, "What's the next line?"

And about sixty of them shouted the line out.

> "Then it's not much of a bleedin' replacement, is it?"

TERRY G   *Mixed feelings, it was mechanical for me, vomit and bananas, all the things I had to do, never gave me the buzz it gave the others. We'd done it long enough, one last bash…people I hadn't seen in years were there, people from my past.*

TERRY J   It was kind of a party, because you sit in little boxes and everybody'd have their picnics out and everything like that and they're all smoking. I had to go out through the audience for the "Albatross" sketch, you know, and you went through all this marijuana smoke.

> "It's a typical Hollywood audience, Bruce. All the kids
> are on drugs and all the adults are on roller skates."

MICHAEL   **So being at the Hollywood Bowl, very nice, very comfortable, lovely glasses of wine at the end of the show, the Rolling Stones, people coming backstage, individual limousines to take us back to anywhere we wanted in Beverley Hills.**

ERIC   Oh, the Bowl was great. I mean it was just the best time. I mean we all got on well, we knew the show, we'd done the show in New York, we'd done the show throughout Canada, we'd done the show throughout England, so we were pretty much on top of the show. It was a crazy experience, four nights at the Bowl, there's eight thousand people. I mean it was just nuts and they were just there to have a good time and we had a good time with them and we gave them an excuse for a good time and it was wonderful. George Harrison was there and Harry Nilsson and Marty Feldman and we had a lot of parties.

GRAHAM   As we fluoresced our way westward along Sunset, past a shimmering Chateau Marmont, another limo glowed alongside. Its sunroof slid back and a figure stood up to wave cheerily at some ladies with long legs standing outside the Body Shop. It was Eric Idle. I pressed the "raise" button on my armrest and went up to the sundeck position. Eric had disappeared inside. I told the driver to get me his number and picked up the handset. Seconds later I heard the phone ring in the next-door car. After the usual pleasantries of "Hello, Eric," "Hello, Graham, what are you on?" had been exchanged, he, Ricky F'Tang, and Penelope Elm crossed over on their limo-loader. "Would you all like to come to a party at my place later on?" I asked, as I passed round a brown paper bag filled with cookies and poured them large vodkas on the rocks.

"I think we're already at one," replied Eric.

"George said he'd try to drop by and I know Harry and Ringo are going to be there later."

"All right, see you later," said Eric. "It's okay if we bring Keith and Ron isn't it?"

"Sure – okay see you later, I'm just going to nip off down through 'Boystown' on the way back – I want to pick up some 'Zoom'..."

"I bet that's not all..." twinkled Eric.

ERIC   John had a good time too, I think, at the Hollywood Bowl. It think everybody was having a good time getting on.

JOHN   And doing it for four nights, balmy weather, wonderful crowds. I understood the rock concert thing then, and I enjoyed every minute of it, and had a wonderful time.

ERIC   I just remember it as a great party. I mean it was a great party and everybody came backstage and there were, you know, nice people, young people, famous people. It was just good times.

NANCY   *And it was sort of historical at that stage, looking back. We did the Hollywood Round, I remember Steve Martin hosted a party for them, and it was terrific in the end because so many people felt so positive about Python. They all felt they'd discovered them. It was excellent.*

CAROL Various celebrities, all the crème de la crème of the Hollywood world, were there and had parties for us. Steve Martin, a great fan of Python, held a big party for us, which I remember well because his house was all white. Everything white. You go into the lounge and it's like going into an art gallery, because there's all these amazing paintings on the wall, and you think, Oh yes, okay, recognise that one. Nothing else except one tree going up the centre of the room, going up, out through the ceiling – very strange.

But what I do remember about this particular party is that Michael was sitting by the pool, just dangling his feet in the water, and there were all these young Hollywood nymphettes who want to break into Hollywood giggling in their little mini teensy weensy bikinis and this one girl was dying to get Michael's attention so she just jumped in the water right in front of him and then came up right in front of him and mysteriously her bikini had just dropped off and she was naked. And it was always Michael they picked. Michael would just go, Mmmm, and not know what to do about it.

GRAHAM It was dark as I and a few guests I'd found en route, at a party in the Polo Lounge – a young Texan, an Irish choirboy, and a Thai busboy called "Bum," among them – arrived back at 203 Bristol Avenue North. Van Dyke Parkes greeted me with "We all love your style, Graham, and to me that's as important as ducks in June."

ERIC There was a party that Graham Chapman threw at his house, and all the Stones came. And it got to be ten o'clock and Graham's mum and dad were there and they came and said, "It's ten o'clock now" and the Stones went, "Oh sorry, sorry love," and they all left because it was ten o'clock at night.

GRAHAM It must have been something I'd eaten; the house seemed to be full of an assemblage of images, sounds and smells and other sensations, mediated through a spot two inches behind the nape of my neck and all the way up the inside of my trousers. I stared at people, hoping that they wouldn't notice how strange they looked to me: Normally this did not bother me. I'd probably been smoking too much...Harry Nilsson was at the piano performing a duet with a barking robot-dog. Ringo then led a rendition of "Happy Birthday to You" accompanied by twenty-five lead vocalists who just happened to be there. Harry and Marty Feldman added a touch of Keith Moon by using the top of the piano as a drum kit. My mother and father hovered in a state of enlightened astonishment at having found yet another black man who was "very well spoken, you know." Taking a cue from Marty, who was by now chasing a Hollywood psychiatrist around the room, trying to embarrass him with a French kiss, I chatted up the nearest sex symbol, Sylvia Kristel, telling her to pop in and see Bernard McKenna, who I felt needed a sexual threat to slow down his rapidly developing affair with a gallon of bourbon. She returned a few moments later, her advances having been repelled by an in-flight ashtray. She wandered off into the garden to be consoled by a girlfriend. Tony Stratton-Smith, first earl of

Lambourn-elect, schoonered past beatifically murmuring mantrillically, "Ah Brazil, Ah Brazil, Ah Brazil…" George Harrison, an island of purity, glowed nearby with a "Hello Graham" and a self-realization-fellowship wave. My mother didn't think that Ronnie Wood and Keith Richard should have been allowed into my bedroom since they were Eric's guests and she was very worried about whether "those two girls were all right out there in the bushes." Loretta Feldman told a bemused Eric how full of shit people could be in an explanatory bellow, Elton John appeared without his cap and spectacles, a bubbling liberated pauntly soul…

Image followed image until early morning: The house was almost empty but the drumming at the piano had resumed and continued until near dawn when Marty and Loretta left, leaving Harry Nilsson, who couldn't understand people's lack of stamina and called me a shit as I saw him firmly to his limo – "Yes, I am" seemed the appropriate reply. Out there at 6:30 A.M. he screamed at the top of his voice in the direction of Hollywood, exclaiming that it too was full of shit. I bellowed in agreement with my friend, as his limo "thhffed" off down the drive towards the rising sun.

TERRY J   Gabriel García Márquez, Lord Lucan, and Geoffrey Chaucer came and stood at the end of my bed and sang extracts from the telephone directory. I couldn't see them very clearly because of the crowds of ice hockey champions trampling over my coverlets, and the B59 bomber that had just landed accidentally on my nose. Something was wrong, and yet it all seemed perfectly normal because this was, after all, LA.

NANCY   *The audience were totally swept away. It was the way Americans completely fell in love with the Beatles the first time they saw them. I think this was the comedy equivalent. It wasn't the overwhelming instant millions-of-dollars-pouring-their-way kind of success, but it was a wonderful revolution of its own kind.*

I think we all had the feeling they'd never do the stage show again…It was like a big Python finale.

Piss Off!! love – Monty Python

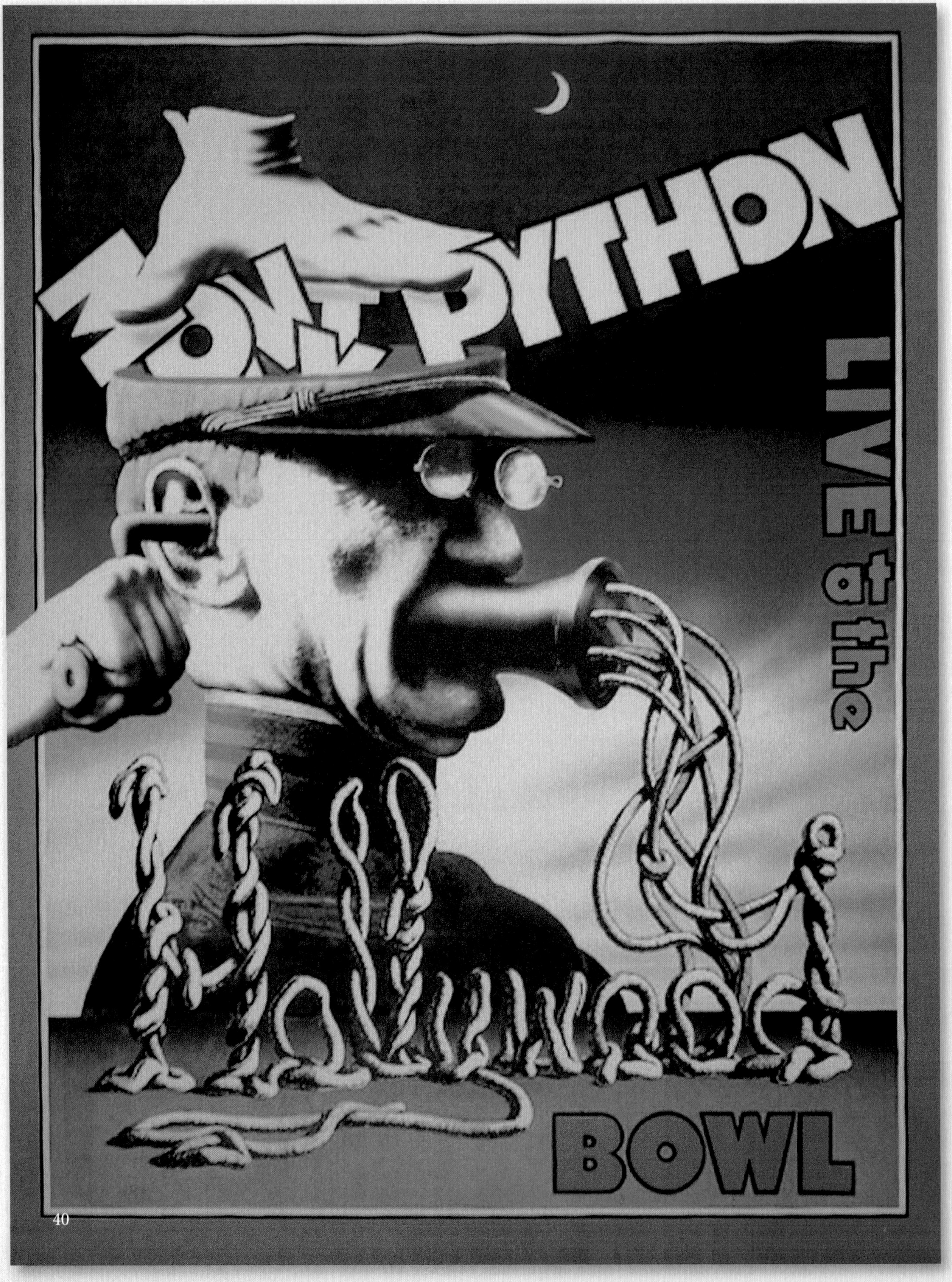
PYTHON
LIVE at the
HOLLYWOOD
BOWL

OFFICIAL PROGRAMME

MONTY PYTHON
AT THE HOLLYWOD BOWL

About the Programme
by Biggles

Hello! You know, flying over the Baltic in a twin-engined
Dragon Rapide can be a bally lonely business, even with
chums like Algy and Ginger prancing around, and its at
times like that when a chap needs the zany, whacky,
kooky, oddball humour of Monty Python to keep his
hands on the joystick. Take this programme (which I'm
sure you have, seeing as they're **FREE!** 20p - Ed.) its a
deuced clever little number and I'm bally proud to have
been asked to explain it. So, here goes..bombs away...no
Algy!..Algy love...Algy!..I meant it metaphorically...
..no, Algy love....Algy!..Al—oh well, teach the Swedes to be neutral.

1. Take the programme in the right hand (end of the right
   arm, right hand side of the body) and grip the other side
   firmly with the left hand (identical to the right hand, but
   on your left as you stand facing the wall), holding the
   joystick firm with your knees.

2. Keeping an eye on the altimeter (3rd one along, next to
   the vanity mirror), fold the programme carefully along
   the vertical perforations, and then..Ginger get off!..then
   carefully fold again along the horizontal perforations.

3. Now you should have a neat, sixteen page souvenir programme, easy to read and easy to assemble, even while
   flying a Dragon Rap...Oh my God! What the hell's
   ALGY! A—

Songs

Part One

"I'm in love with Pisso" .... Puss
"J'Aime Pisso" .... Puss (reprise)
"I've got a Heartful of Love" .... Pisso*
"Isn't life wonderful, apart from VAT" .... All
"Sod you, Warfarin" .... Depravo the Rat
"Just Another One" .... Pisso
"The Retreat from Moscow" .... The Arthur Condom Babes

Part Two

"That's Surgery" .... Simon the Vet
"I love you with all my heart and lungs" .... Puss
"It's great to be Jewish" .... All

* Not suitable for children.

Dance routines by Dyno-Rod.
Cigarettes by Imperial Slow-Death Company.
Mr. Gilliams sausages by 'My-man' Pork Boutique.
Mr. Chapman's overdraft by NatWest.
Mr. Jones' fish by "Act 'n Fish" of Drury Lane.
Mr. Palin's toupee by "Never-Kno" Toupees
Miss Cleveland's body stocking by Mr. Cleese.
Mr. Idle's posture by "The Actor's Friend".
Mr. Cleese's Wigs by "You Bitch" of Bond Street.
Jokes constructed by British Scaffolding.
Mr. Gilliam's ointment for the little rash on his bottom by: Associated Pharmaceuticals.

Marijuana by 'Q' Division
Mr. Chapman's throat-spray by International Vintners.
Leopards by London Zoo
Zulu Warriors by Vorster Theatrical Supplies.
The Battle On The Ice by Frigidaire
Brains by Currys
Internal Protection by Dyno-Rod

Neil Innes appears by permission of the National Film Archive

Monty Python would like to thank the vicar for the use of the Hall.

GRAHAM CHAPMAN, 19

is the youngest member of the group. A modest, soft-spoken Dubliner. A brilliant and prolific writer, Graham feels that without him the show would have been a complete disaster. A brilliant and prolific writer, Graham wrote many of the I.T.M.A. Shows as well as most of E.M. Forster. Graham's favourite colour is off-white and his favourite heavy gas is Helium.

JOHN CLEESE, 18

is even younger than Graham, the youngest of the group. John refers to himself as a comic genius, a manic wild-eyed wizard of wit, and one of the most popular men since Ghandi. His special role in Python, he feels, has been the complete integration of writing and performing into a viable and successful whole. John's favourite colour is fish, and his pet hate is insincerity.

ERIC IDLE, 13

is even younger than Graham Chapman and John Cleese. Eric is the real genius of the group. Much taller than a midget, Eric is, as he puts it, "little short of brilliant". Eric has brought to Python much of the anarchic humour and brilliantly surrealist performance which would have been so sadly lacking without him. Eric was born under Derry and Toms.

CAST
in order of appearance

PRINCE DANDINI (A nobleman's son) .... Lyn Ashley
PUSS .... John Cleese
BALTHAZAR (A rich merchant) .... Michael Palin
PRINCESS BALDRUBADOR ...... Terry Jones and Graham Chapman
THE EMPEROR OF PEKING .... Eric Idle
PISSO, The Alcoholic Dog .... Himself
WIDOW TANKEY .... Marlon Brando*
HONEST JACK (A friend of Puss's) .... Terry Gilliam
DEPRAVO THE RAT (A friend of Pisso's) .... Himself
FAIRY SUNSHINE .... Neil Innes
RHONDA (Puss's physiotherapist) .... Mrs. S. Baldwin
MING .... The Policemen ...... Det/Sgt Arnold, Special Patrol Squad.
                      Regional Crime Squad, Special Assignments
                      Division, C.I.D.
MONG .... Detective Chief Superintendent Wilson
SIMON THE VET (The man who neutered Puss) .... Eric Idle**
FILTHY PHILIP, the Unhygienic Hedgehog, (The man who
        first had Puss, and a friend of
        Pisso's) .... Sir Laurence Bolivier
ANDY THE TURK .... All

With

The Titan Drilling And Off-Shore Exploration Company Dancers
The Arthur Condom Babes, the Trio Los Cheapos — still at pre-VAT
prices, and The Amazing Berg Fegg々×2 —A Death-defying High-Wire
Act.

* If wet, this part will be taken by Terry Jones and Graham Chapman.
** If wet, this part will be taken by Stevie Wonder ***.
*** If a bit muggy, but not actually wet, this part will be taken by
Depravo the Rat.

Order of Scenes

Part One

One .... The Sultan's Palace
Two .... On the Way to Abdul's Cave
Three .... On the Way Back to Abdul's Cave
Four .... Right up against Abdul's Cave
Five .... Half in Abdul's Cave
Six .... Entirely in Abdul's Cave (except for the fingers)
Seven .... Lunch

Interval

Part Two

One ...... Princess Baldrubador's boudoir (really Abdul's Cave)
Two .... Pisso's Kennel*
Three .... Abdul's Flat in Leeds
Four .... At the door of Abdul's Flat in Leeds
Five ..... In the diner/kitchenette of Abdul's Flat in Leeds
Six .... The Fairy Circle
Seven .... The Fairy Grotto
Eight .... The Fairies are Arrested
Nine .... At the Vet's*
Ten .... The Haunted Sauna
Eleven .... The Grand Finale (if wet, in Pisso's Kennel*)
Suitable for Children.

43

The Python Story

The MONTY PYTHON team met while serving with the R.A.F. in the last war. They were all attached to the now legendary and effeminate 243 squadron which flew over 400 difficult missions over Europe dropping tons of make-up to the Allied troops.

After the war they all wore very loose suits, and met up again at an R.A.F. reunion in 1947. There the idea first came up for "a whacky, new kind of show to take the lid off all the sacred cows of everything in Britain". After explaining their idea to the top brass at the BBC the boys were given jobs as commissionaires in the newly-extended car park at Alexandra Palace. But it wasn't long before "Doc", Chapman and Terry "Pud" Jones left the group to become robbers. The others stayed on at the BBC until 1953 when they all met up again at an R.A.F. reunion in Petts Wood. After a few creme-de-menthes at the bar Eric "Tadger" Idle sat behind the piano and started to tap out the first notes of a tune that was to revolutionise the whole history of television. As the boys began to sing along, a tall distinguished figure at an opposite table began to sit up and listen. It was, none other than Hugh, now Sir Hugh Carleton — Greene, soon to become one of the most powerful figures in British post-war television. If he hadn't left in such a hurry as the boys began to sing, their careers might have been very different.

In the late 50's Mike 'Smudger' Palin and Terry "Please don't kick me when I'm Down and Out" Gilliam left the BBC to run an R.A.F. Benevolent home near Hove and it was here on a wintry day that a chance meeting of a few old service buddies was to lead to a breakthrough which was to influence so many millions of people in later years.

But still Python was a long way off and it wasn't until a Bring Back Flogging Dinner Dance at Esher in 1966 that the boys came up with an idea that was to change everything. They decided to rejoin the R.A.F. Two glorious years followed in which the boys saw much of the active and varied life which lies in store for all R.A.F. recruits. After a moving passing-out ceremony beneath the tower at R.A.F. Cranwell which has meant so much to generations of men who gave everything to fight for the freedom of Britain's skies, the boys left to do Monty Python.

I am over 21 and don't like girls much.

I am interested in joining the Luftwaffe
R.A.F.
R.C.M.P.

40
for not less than 50 years.
65

Signature ....

THE CAVES of PASSION
by Eunice Von Papen

THE STORY SO FAR

Helga, a young attractive German student, has come over to a finishing school in England. As more and more of her is finished she falls under the spell of the sinister Dr. Wang, the local Datsun dealer. At one of his pre-launch sales parties she meets Wing Lu, the South-East area Datsun co-ordinator. He declares his love for her, and says he can get her things on discount. George and Kruger, meanwhile, decide to press on with their plan to assassinate the royal family, declare England a republic, and really sort out a Prices & Incomes policy that worked.

44

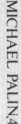
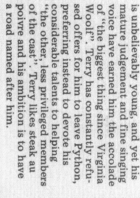

TERRY JONES, 12

is unbelievably young, and yet his mature judgement and fine singing voice have earned him the accolade of "the biggest thing since Virginia Woolf". Terry has constantly refused offers for him to leave Python, preferring instead to devote his considerable talents to helping "the other, less privileged members of the cast". Terry likes steak au poivre and his ambition is to have a road named after him.

TERRY GILLIAM, 10½

is the real baby of the group. He is so young and talented that it is almost presumption to mention his name along with the others. "I think I can safely say that without me there would have been no Monty Python, no United Nations and quite possibly no end to the Second World War", says Terry disarmingly. Terry has written over 40 symphonies and his greatest likes are his own cartoons and having his inside leg measured.

MICHAEL PALIN, 4

is the Python superstar. A brilliant humourist, Michael is the vital creative influence without whom Python could not have survived. With an I.Q. of several thousand, Michael still finds time to look up people who owe him money. Michael drives a scarlet and gold Lamborghini or else hitchhikes.

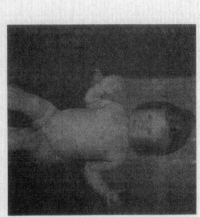

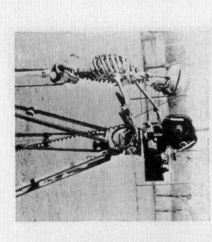

CAROL CLEVELAND, 19

is, along with Graham Chapman, the youngest member of the group. Carol met the group at Shepherd's Bush Police Station and has been with them ever since. Carole's favourite insect is the Angolan Termite and her starsign is Basil.

NEIL WINSTON INNES, over 70

is over 70, and has been playing the piano since before the Renaissance. Amongst his hits have been "Urban Spaceman", and amongst other people's hits have been "Tell Laura I Love Her", "Bird Dog" and "My Kind of Guy". Neil's favourite colour is either green or blue, and his hobby is joinery.

IAN MACNAUGHTON

who directed the film in this show and the original Python T.V. Shows, is one of the few youngsters on a pension. Ian hails from Helensburgh, near Glasgow — too far for most people to hear him — and spotted the Python team at a jumble sale. Ian's favourite colour is brown, with a little ice, and he's a keen Scottish Naturist.

45

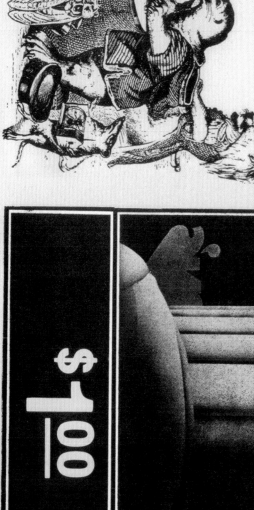

What To Do After The Show

1. If you have been injured or maimed at all during the Show, go straight to hospital. Find a nurse or qualified doctor (make them produce a certificate if in doubt) and point out to them the places on your body where you have been injured or maimed. Do not fondle any of the medical people, unless they specifically request you to do so, and unless there are washing facilities nearby.

   Under no circumstances should you go to the cinema first, or have a lobster bhuna with chapatis and mango chutney yum yum.

2. If you have been very seriously Maimed or Injured during the Show, you will want to get to hospital as quickly as possible. This can be done on a bus. I don't know the numbers of the buses to the nearest hospital, but you could ask an usherette or the lady at the cash desk. She will also tell you where the nearest bus stop is. Try not to drop blood on the theatre carpet. And do try not to rub curry into your wounds or even nice chapatis.

3. If your injuries are worse than at first you realised, you won't realise at first, but when you do realise, as soon as the curtain comes down, rush for the exit and be ill outside — you'll be doing your bit to help us keep these theatres nice and clean.

4. In case of severe injury that at first seems worse than it is and then later seems better, but is in fact even worse, don't waste any time, go straight to the Front of House Manager and try to explain it to him. He will sort it out for you, and incidentally he could also confirm what I was saying about Meat Vindaloo.

5. Should you by any chance have sustained no injuries during the Show, for heavens sake don't go round crowing about it. After all there's nothing so wonderful about not being injured — thousands of people go to the theatre every day without being injured or even bruised about the head. In fact, in a well-run, electrically-lit, modern theatre there is probably as much chance of you escaping physical injury as anywhere in the Free World.*

6. Above all don't go running home and telling everybody how many people got injured. This Show is perfectly safe, and there is no real need to wear protective clothing at all.

* Not including Madras.

$1⁰⁰

Episode 19: AT THE CLINIC

Helga recognised him straightaway — it was Emerhard Von Atkins the most brilliant surgeon in Europe. So these were the hands that had cleared up Bismarck's skin complaint.

"Let's have a little look" said Von Atkins and his skilful, healing hands played confidently over Helga's young body.

Helga left for London in desperation quite unaware of the awful plot Kruger was hatching.

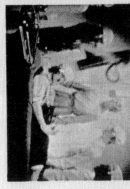

"I've come about my brother," she said. "He's been learning the piano, for nine years but still seems to have difficulty mastering it, my father and mother are distraught for they are both great concert pianists, as are his uncles."

Von Atkins decided to operate on the spot, even though the patient wasn't there. They operated instead on one of his colleagues, Herr. Murder. It was to be the first-ever brain-knee transplant and needed all the skills of this great and zany man.

On the boat she met the elegant and mysterious Sapper Eden — little did she know that one day he would become the greatest Minister of Health Britain ever had.

That night at a gin rummy party in the padres cabin, Herr Eden introduced her to several of his friends — Herr Stafford Cripps, Herr Baldwin and Herr Harold Nicholson.

Leaving her frail old wreck of a mother to make her own way to the Ball, Helga went into town.

Once in London she met her mother in Derry and Toms and with the help of a most personable assistant they tried on some gowns for the Coronation night Ball — to be held that very evening at 14B Ferraris Buildings (Top Bell).

Suddenly Helga noticed that one of the royal Guards of Honour was behaving very oddly. He seemed to be signalling.

She looked again and sure enough it was Sapper Eden aiming at the Queen

Next Week: Helga has a colostomy, Kruger finds his plans foiled and his office chair mysteriously wet.

The royal procession was wending its way through the crowd filled streets. The Queen looked radiant, her husband looked radiant and her private detective looked radiant.

47

How to Walk Silly

The Llama

Four Spanish guitarists play a frenetic burst of flamenco.
A Spanish Looney in evening dress runs in.

LOONEY

Senores senoras y senoritas. Buenas noches. Esta noche presentamos con mucho gusto informacion interesante aperca de Llama.

On screen are various silly pictures of llamas.
The guitarists play another frenetic burst of flamenco.

Enter an attractive female in a spangled Magician's Assistant costume and a weird man in a long raincoat with "Eat More Pork" on his back.
They display subtitles on large caption boards at either side of stage.

LOONEY

La llama es un cuadrupedo!

SUBTITLE

The llama is a quadruped!

LOONEY

Que vive en los grandes rios como el Amazonas

SUBTITLE

Which lives in big rivers like the Amazon

GUITARISTS

(*burst of flamenco*)
Amazonas!

LOONEY

Tiene dos Orejas, un Corazon

SUBTITLE

It has two ears, a heart

LOONEY

Una frente y un pico para camer miel.

SUBTITLE

A forehead and a beak for eating honey.

A frenetic burst of flamenco as the Looney produces a trick flower from his coat.

ALL

Ole!

LOONEY

Pero esta provisita de aletas pana nader

SUBTITLE

But it is provided with fins for swimming.

GUITARISTS

(Singing)

Las llamas son mas grandes que las ranas

SUBTITLE

Llamas are lager than frogs.

LOONEY

Llamas son peligrosas y si usted ve una llama

SUBTITLE

Llamas are dangerous so if you see one…

LOONEY

Donde hay gente nadando, Usted grita

SUBTITLE

Where people are swimming, you shout…

LOONEY

Cuidado Llamas!

SUBTITLE

Look out, there are llamas

LOONEY AND GUITARISTS

(singing)

Cuidado cuidado cuidado cuidado las llamas!
Cuidado cuidado cuidado cuidado las llamas!

A man in a Spanish dress and mantilla drives in on a moped and bursts an inflated paper bag.

ALL

Ole!

Gumby Flower Arranging

Pretty music plays.

VOICE-OVER
And now flower arranging. Mister D.P. Gumby is here to show you how
to arrange flowers.

*A very silly man with granny glasses, a moustache, a collarless shirt, knitted fair isle sweater, gumboots and
a knotted handkerchief on his head.*

GUMBY
Good evening! Tonight flower arranging. First take a bunch of flowers.
Pretty begonias, irises, freesias and chrymanthesums.
Then, arrange them, nicely, in a vase!

He stuffs the bunch of flowers, blooms first into a vase and bashes them in with a wooden mallet, shouting.

Oh get in. Get in!

Two assistants in white coats rush in and hustle him off stage.

Michelangelo and the Pope

A full Renaissance Pope sits on a throne. A Renaissance Choir sing a Gregorian Chant.

SERVANT

A *Michelangelo* to see you, Your Holiness.

POPE

Who?

SERVANT

Michelangelo, the famous Renaissance artist whose best known works include the ceiling of the Sistine Chapel, and the celebrated statue of David…

POPE

Ah. Very well…

SERVANT

In 1514 he returned to Florence and began his career…

POPE

All right, that's enough, they've got it now!

SERVANT

Oh. (*Exits*)

Michelangelo enters in Renaissance costume holding an artist's palette and brushes.

MICHELANGELO

Good evening, Your Holiness.

POPE

Evening, Michelangelo. I want to have a word with you about this painting of yours *The Last Supper*.

MICHELANGELO

Oh, yeah?

POPE

I'm not happy about it.

MICHELANGELO

Oh dear. It took me hours.

POPE

Not happy at all.

MICHELANGELO

Is it the jelly you don't like?

POPE

No.

MICHELANGELO

They do add a bit of color, don't they?
Oh, I know, you don't like the kangaroo?

53

POPE

What kangaroo?

MICHELANGELO

No problem, I'll paint him out.

POPE

I never saw a kangaroo!

MICHELANGELO

He's right in the back. I'll paint him out! No sweat, I'll make him into a Disciple.

POPE

Aah.

MICHELANGELO

All right?

POPE

That's the problem.

MICHELANGELO

What is?

POPE

The Disciples.

MICHELANGELO

Are they too Jewish? I made Judas the most Jewish.

POPE

No, it's just that there are twenty-eight of them.

MICHELANGELO

So another one will never matter. I'll make the kangaroo into another one.

POPE

No, that's not the point.

MICHELANGELO

All right. I'll lose the kangaroo. Be honest, I wasn't perfectly happy with it.

POPE

That's not the point. There are *twenty-eight* Disciples!

MICHELANGELO

Too many?

POPE

Well, of course it's too many!

MICHELANGELO

Yeah, I know that, but I wanted to give the impression of a *real* Last Supper. You know, not just any old Last Supper. Not like a Last Meal or a Final Snack. I wanted to do a real mother of a blowout.

POPE

There were only *twelve* Disciples at the Last Supper.

MICHELANGELO

Well, maybe some of the others came along afterwards for a drink?

POPE

There were only *twelve* altogether.

MICHELANGELO

Maybe some of their friends dropped in?

POPE

Look! There were just *twelve* Disciples and our Lord at the Last Supper. The Bible clearly says so.

MICHELANGELO

No friends?

POPE

No friends.

MICHELANGELO

Waiters?

POPE

No.

MICHELANGELO

Cabaret?

POPE

No!

MICHELANGELO

You see, I like them, they help to flesh out the scene. I could lose a few, I suppose but…

POPE

Look! There were only *twelve* Disciples at…

MICHELANGELO

I've got it! We'll call it *The Last But One Supper*.

POPE

What?

MICHELANGELO

Well there must have been one, if there was a *Last* Supper there must have been a one before that, so this, is *The Penultimate Supper*! The Bible doesn't say how many people were there, does it?

POPE

No, but…

MICHELANGELO

Well there you are, then!

POPE

Look! The Last Supper is a significant event in the life of our Lord, The Penultimate Supper was not! Even if they had a conjurer and a mariachi band.

MICHELANGELO

Oo.

POPE

Now, a Last Supper I commissioned from you, and a Last Supper I want! With *twelve* Disciples and *one* Christ!

MICHELANGELO

One?

POPE

Yes one! Now will you please tell me what in God's name possessed you to paint this with three Christs in it?

MICHELANGELO

It works, mate!

POPE

Works?

MICHELANGELO

Yeah! It looks great! The fat one balances the two skinny ones.

POPE

There was only *one* Redeemer!

MICHELANGELO

I know that, we all know that, but what about a bit of artistic license?

POPE

One Messiah is what I want!

MICHELANGELO

I'll tell you what you want, mate! You want a bloody photographer! That's what you want. Not a bloody creative artist!

POPE

I'll tell you what I want! I want a Last Supper with *one* Christ, *twelve* disciples, *no* kangaroos, *no* trampoline acts, by Thursday lunch, or you don't get paid!

MICHELANGELO

Bloody fascist!

POPE

Look! I'm the bloody Pope! I may not know much about art, but I know what I like!

International Wrestling

A wrestling ring.
A Referee is waiting patiently.
A Ring Announcer in evening dress addresses the mike.

RING ANNOUNCER

Hello, good evening and welcome to All-In Wrestling, brought to you tonight, ladies and gentlemen, by the makers of Scum, the world's first ever combined hair oil, foot ointment, and salad dressing. And by the makers of Titan, the novelty nuclear missile! You never know when it'll go off! Surprise your friends, amuse your enemies, start the party with a bang! Introducing, ladies and gentlemen, all the way from a Mud Wrestling Tour of the OPEC countries…in the red corner: Colin "Bomber" Harris!

Colin in wrestling kit bounds into the ring and acknowledges the crowd.

…and, in the blue corner…all the way from a Mud Wrestling tour of the OPEC countries…Colin "Bomber" Harris!

Colin raises his hand and acknowledges the crowd.

Well, now, ladies and gentlemen, this is the first time that Colin "Bomber" Harris has met himself. And he's perfectly matched, the same height and the same weight so this should be a very close bout. A few words from the referee and any moment now we'll be ready for the start of Round One.

Bell rings

And there goes the bell!

Colin begins to wrestle with himself.

Colin moves to the middle of the ring and he's looking for an opening, going for the handhold…He's got it! Into the head squeeze… The head squeeze is a favorite move of Colin's. And there he's used the flying buttock to get him into the missionary position and already Colin is working on that weak left knee of his! A half nelson…a half nelson and a Philadelphia sandwich and oh dear Colin bit himself on purpose there! And

yes, I thought so, he has been given a public warning by the referee! And Colin is incensed with that! He did not like that one little bit! And he's looking to quickly get back at himself. A double overhead nostril…and an O'Brien kickback into the Boston crayfish, no, it's the Boston cuttlefish, or is it the langoustine? No, it's the Lobster Thermidor!

Colin manages to pin himself with his shoulders to the canvas.

And Colin has caught himself by surprise and yes it's the first fall to Colin "Bomber" Harris! And Colin must be pretty pleased with himself having put himself into that one! Now then, a Strawberry Whip, a Vanilla Whip, a Chocolate Whip…and there it is, Colin's most famous hold: the one-neck-over-the-shoulder clutch and Colin's in real trouble! He's just made it to the rope…just a little lucky there…and there is a double Eydie Gormé, which he should be able to twist out of and he does…but he's looking pretty groggy…and I think he's caught himself.

Colin smashes himself on the chin with his forearm until he falls to the floor.

Oh my word, the forearm smash and – Colin "Bomber" Harris has knocked himself out and so he is the winner and he goes on next week to meet himself in the final!

The Silly Olympics

COMMENTATOR

Hello, and welcome to Munich, for the 27th Silly Olympiad, an event held traditionally every 3.7 years, which this year has brought together competitors from over 4 million different countries. And here we are at the start of the first event of the afternoon: the second semi-final of the 100 Meters for People with No Sense of Direction.

On the track a field of Runners begin to get into their blocks for the 100 Meters.

And there are the competitors; Lane One: Kolomovski of Poland; Lane Two: Zatapatique of France; Lane Three: Gropovich of the United States; next to him: Drabble of Trinidad; next to him: Fernandez of Spain; and in the outside lane: Bormann of Brazil!

STARTER

Get set!

The Starter fires his pistol:

Bang!

All the Competitors race off in totally different directions.

COMMENTATOR

Well, that was fun, wasn't it? And now, over to the other end of the stadium where we're waiting for the start of the 1500 Meters for the Deaf. And they're under starter's orders.

The Starter fires his pistol:

Bang!

Nobody moves. The Starter fires again:

Bang!

Still nobody moves.

And we'll be coming back the moment there's any action. And now over to the swimming.

2nd VOICE

And you join us here at the Bundesabsurd pool just in time to see the start of the 200 Meters Freestyle for Non-swimmers. Watch for the Australian champion Ron Barnett in the second lane.

Swimmers on their starting blocks.
The Starter blows his whistle.
The Swimmers all dive into the pool, but sadly they do not re-emerge.

2nd VOICE
Well, we'll be bringing you back the moment they start fishing the corpses out.

COMMENTATOR
And now over to the start of the Marathon for Incontinents. Forty-four competitors from twenty-nine different countries, all of them with the most superbly weak bladders. Not a tight sphincter in sight. Ready to embark, nevertheless, on the world's longest race and they're just aching to go!

A large crowd of Marathon Runners are limbering up.

STARTER
On your marks! Get set!

The Starter fires his pistol:

Bang!

COMMENTATOR
And they're off!

All the Competitors race into a door marked "Gents."

Well, back at the 1500 Meters for the Deaf and the starter's putting up a magnificent show!

The Starter is still firing his pistol. The Competitors still do not move.

We've had scattered fire, random fire, and now ceremonial firing, but still nothing from the hard of hearing. It's enough to make you chew your own foot off!

And now the high jump! Katerina Ovelenski from the Soviet Union! And what a jump! What a jump! She's leapt over King Ludwig's Castle of Neuschwanstein.

That ought to be a record!

And here we are at the 3000-Meter Steeplechase for People Who Think They Are Chickens!

A steeplechase course. Several Competitors are clucking, flapping their elbows and behaving like chickens.

There's Samuelson of the United States, and over there is Klaus of East Germany! He's been broody for the last three Olympics.

Klaus is perched on one of the obstacles, flapping his arms. There are three eggs beneath him.

There's the leader, Abe Seagull of Canada, who's made a very good start. Poor Scott laid an egg at the water jump, and has now gone completely loopy.

61

The Marathon runners are now running down a long woodland trail.

> And now we are back with the Marathon for Incontinents once again. There's Polanski of Poland in the lead.

Polanski runs into the bushes to take a leak.

> ...and now Brewer of Australia is taking over!

But he too cannot hold it and runs off the road for a pee.

> And so now it is Alvarez of Cuba, followed by the Norwegian Bjorg...

They both run off desperately into the trees. More runners follow them.

> Well, these must be some of the weakest bladders ever to represent their countries!

World Forum

PRESENTER

Good evening. Tonight on World Forum we are deeply privileged to have with us Karl Marx, the founder of modern socialism and author of *The Communist Manifesto*…

Karl Marx nods.

Vladimir Ilyich Ulyanov, better known to the world as Lenin, leader of the Russian Revolution, writer, statesman, and father of modern socialism…

Lenin nods.

Che Guevara, the Bolivian guerilla leader…

Che is smoking a cigar.

and Mao Tse-tung, chairman of the Chinese Communist Party since 1949.

Mao nods.

And the first question is for you, Karl Marx. "The Hammers." "The Hammers" is the nickname of what English football team?

Marx hasn't a clue.

"The Hammers." No? Well, bad luck, Karl. It is, in fact, West Ham United. Now, Che Guevara. Che. Coventry City last won the English FA Cup in what year?

Che too has no clue.

No? I can throw the question open. Anybody else? Coventry City last won the English FA Cup in what year?

None of them have any idea what he is talking about.

No? Well I'm not surprised you didn't get that. It is in fact a trick question. Coventry City have *never* won the English FA Cup! So now with the scores all even, it's on to Round Two, and Lenin, your Starter for 10. Jerry Lee Lewis has had over seventeen major solid gold hits in the U.S. of A. What's the name of the biggest? Jerry Lee Lewis's solid gold biggie? No?

Mao Tse-tung presses his buzzer.

Yes, Mao Tse-tung?

MAO TSE-TUNG

"Great Balls of Fire"?

PRESENTER

Yes, it was indeed! Very well challenged. And now we come on to our third round. Our contestant tonight is Karl Marx and our special prize is this beautiful lounge suite!

Behind him on the screen is a three-piece suite.

AUDIENCE

Oooh!

The Presenter takes Karl Marx and moves him into a spotlight.

PRESENTER

Karl has elected to answer questions on Workers' Control of Factories, so here we go with question number one. You, nervous, Karl?

Karl nods.

Just a little. Well, never mind pal, have a go! *(Reads a card)* "The development of the industrial proletariat is conditioned by what other development?"

Karl thinks.

"The development of the industrial proletariat is conditioned by what *other* development?"

KARL MARX
The development of the industrial bourgeoisie.

PRESENTER
Good! Yes, it is indeed! Well done, Karl! You're on your way to a lounge suite! Now, Karl, question number two. *(Reads)* "The struggle of class against class is a *what* struggle?"

KARL MARX
A political struggle.

PRESENTER
One final question, and that beautiful lounge suite will be yours! Ready, Karl? You're a brave man. Your final question: Who won the English FA Cup in 1949?

KARL MARX
Er, the workers' control of the means of production? The struggle of the urban proletariat?

PRESENTER
No, it was Wolverhampton Wanderers who beat Leicester 3–1.

KARL MARX
Oh, shit!

PRESENTER
Never mind. No one leaves this show empty-handed, so we're going to cut off your hands.

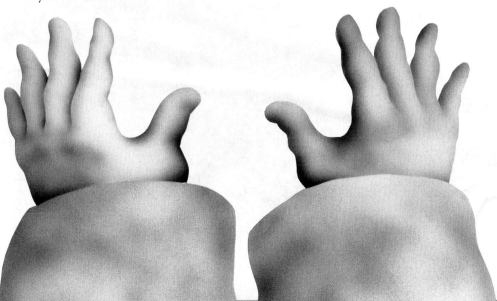

The Ministry of Silly Walks

A drab office with a desk and hat stand. A rather dull little man is sitting nervously waiting.

The Director enters with a bowler hat on. He has a very silly walk and it takes him forever to take his hat off, hang it on the peg, put down his briefcase and sit down behind his desk.

DIRECTOR

Good morning. I'm sorry to have kept you waiting, but I'm afraid my walk has become rather silly over the last three months, so it does take me rather longer to get to the office.

Finally he gets to his chair and sits down.

Now, what was it again?

APPLICANT

Well sir, I have got a silly walk and I'd like to obtain government backing to help me develop it.

DIRECTOR

I see. May I see this silly walk of yours?

APPLICANT

Oh, yes, certainly.

The applicant gets up and demonstrates a rather pathetic silly walk.

DIRECTOR

Yes, I see, that's it, is it?

APPLICANT

Ah, well, yes, that's it.

DIRECTOR

Yes, yes, yes. It's not *particularly* silly, is it?

APPLICANT

Well, er…

DIRECTOR

I mean, the left leg isn't silly at all and the right leg merely does a double O'Brien half turn every alternate step.

APPLICANT

Yes, but I feel with a government grant I could make it a lot more silly.

DIRECTOR

Mr. Stanford, the very real problem is public expenditure…

The Director rises and walks around the room in a very silly fashion.

You see, the Ministry of Silly Walks is no longer getting the kind of support it needs. There's Defense, National Health, Housing, Education, Social Security, Silly Walks. They're all supposed to get the same. But last year, the government spent *less* on Silly Walks than they did on Industrial Reorganization. We're supposed to get 348 million pounds a year to cover our entire Silly Walks Program. Coffee?

APPLICANT

Yes, please.

DIRECTOR

(*depressing intercom*)

Hello, Mrs. Twolumps, could we have two cups of coffee, please.

MRS. TWOLUMPS

Yes, Mr. Teabag.

DIRECTOR

Mad as a hatter. You see, the Israelis have a man who can take his own left leg off and swallow it with every alternate step, whereas the Japanese, cunning electronically obsessed little…

They both stare at the Secretary as she comes in with a very silly walk which splashes the coffee all over the tray.

Yes, thank you, Mrs. Twolumps. Lovely.

She exits.

You're interested in Silly Walks, aren't you?

APPLICANT

Rather!

DIRECTOR

Right, well, take a look at this then!

Silly walks on film.

The Bruces

Three Australians in bush outfits with wide-brimmed hats with corks dangling from them.

BRUCE I
Good evening, ladies and Bruces!

BRUCE II
G'day, Bruce.

BRUCE I
G'day, Bruce.

BRUCE III
G'day, Bruce.

BRUCE I
It's very nice to be here this evening! We're all Philosophy professors from the University of Woolamaloo, Australia!

ALL BRUCES
Australia, Australia, Australia! We love ya!

BRUCE I
I teach Hegelian philosophy, Bruce teaches Aristotelian philosophy, and Bruce here is in charge of the sheep dip.

BRUCE II
Bloody thirsty work, Bruce.

BRUCE I
Well why don't you just chuck out a few of these tiny free samples.

They chuck huge cans of Foster's lager into the audience.

All right! Now, the reason we do this, ladies and Bruces, is frankly over here we find your American beer is a little like making love in a canoe!

BRUCE III
Making love in a canoe?

BRUCE I
It's fucking close to water! Well now, we're going to try and raise the tone a little by singing a nice intellectual song for those two or three of you in the audience who understand these things.

BRUCE II
Right!

BRUCE I
So, here we go!

ALL BRUCES

Immanuel Kant was a real pissant
Who was very rarely stable
Heidegger, Heidegger was a boozy beggar
Who could think you under the table
David Hume could out-consume
Schopenhauer and Hegel
And Wittgenstein was a beery swine
Who was just as sloshed as Schlegel
There's nothing Nietszche couldn't teach ya
'Bout the raising of the wrist
Socrates himself was permanently pissed

BRUCE I

Let's hold it a second. I can see some of these Bruces are in a bit of a playful mood tonight. Ain't that true, Bruce?

BRUCE II

Yeah, Bruce.

BRUCE I

Anyway, why don't we get these guys to sing along with us?

BRUCE II

Okay, I've got the words somewhere.

He pulls a very tiny piece of paper out of his shorts and holds it up to the audience.

BRUCE I

Right! Ready!

ALL BRUCES

Immanuel Kant was a real pissant
Who was very rarely stable
Heidegger, Heidegger was a boozy…

The singalong peters out.

BRUCE I

They're a typical American audience, Bruce! All the kids are on drugs, and all the adults are on roller skates! Have we got anything bigger to put the words up for these rather short-sighted people?

The words are lowered on a flat. A female Bruce enters with a pointer.

BRUCE II

This is Bruce from the Biology Department.

BRUCE I

All right. Okay, here we go.

The Bruces lead the Audience in a singalong.

ALL BRUCES

Immanuel Kant was a real pissant
Who was very rarely stable
Heidegger, Heidegger was a boozy beggar
Who could think you under the table
David Hume could out-consume
Schopenhauer and Hegel
And Wittgenstein was a beery swine
Who was just as sloshed as Schlegel

There's nothing Nietzsche couldn't teach ya
'Bout the raising of the wrist
Socrates himself was permanently pissed
John Stuart Mill of his own free will
On half a pint of shandy was particularly ill
Plato they say could stick it away
Half a crate of whiskey every day
Aristotle, Aristotle was a bugger for the bottle
Hobbes was fond of his Dram
And René Descartes was a drunken fart
"I drink, therefore I am !"
Yes Socrates himself is particularly missed
A lovely little thinker
But a bugger when he's pissed!

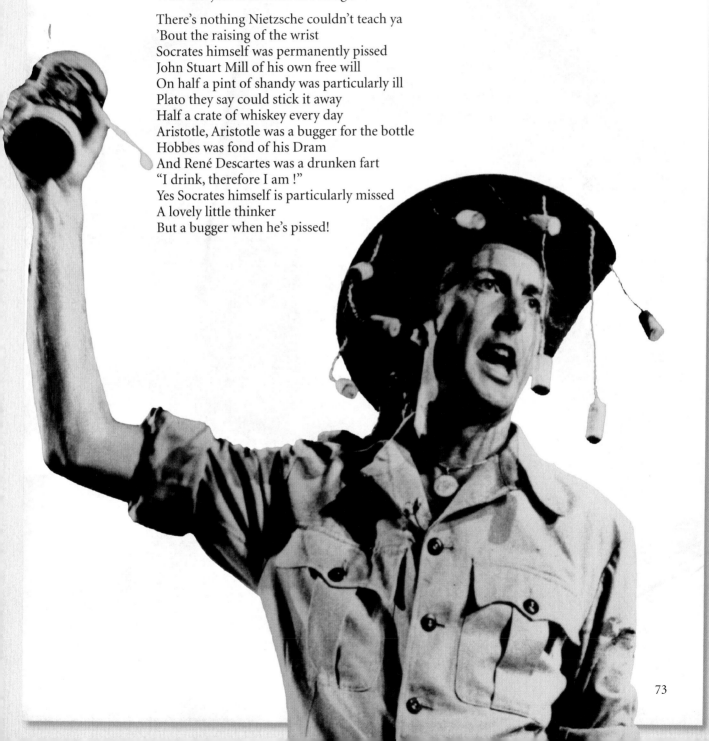

Crunchy Frog

CONSTABLE

Mr. Hilton?

MR. HILTON

Yes.

CONSTABLE

You are sole proprietor and owner of the Whizzo Chocolate Company?

MR. HILTON

I am.

CONSTABLE

Constable Parrot and I are from the Hygiene Squad.

MR. HILTON

Oh, yes.

CONSTABLE

We'd like to have a word with you about your box of chocolates entitled "The Whizzo Quality Assortment."

MR. HILTON

Ah, good, yes.

CONSTABLE

If I may begin at the beginning. First, there is the Cherry Fondue. Now this is extremely nasty, but we can't prosecute you for that!

MR. HILTON

Agreed.

CONSTABLE

Next we have number four "Crunchy Frog."

MR. HILTON

Ah, yes.

CONSTABLE

Am I right in thinking there's a *real* frog in here?

MR. HILTON

Yes, a little one.

CONSTABLE

Is it cooked?

MR. HILTON

No.

CONSTABLE

What? A *raw* frog?

MR. HILTON

We use only the finest baby frogs, dew picked and flown from Iraq, cleansed in the finest quality spring water, lightly killed, and sealed in a treble milk chocolate envelope, and lovingly frosted with glucose!

CONSTABLE

That's as may be, but it's still a frog!

MR. HILTON

What else would it be?

CONSTABLE

You don't even take the bones out?

MR. HILTON

If we took the bones out, it wouldn't be crunchy, would it?

CONSTABLE

Constable Parrot ate one of those!

CONSTABLE PARROT

Would you excuse me for a moment, sir?

CONSTABLE

Yes.

Parrot goes to throw up.

MR. HILTON

Well, it says "Crunchy Frog" quite clearly.

CONSTABLE

Never mind that. We have to protect the public. People aren't going to think there's a *real* frog in chocolate. They're bound to think it's some sort of mock frog.

MR. HILTON

Mock frog? We use no artificial preservatives or additives of any kind!

CONSTABLE

Nevertheless, I advise you in future to change the words "Crunchy Frog" with the legend "Crunchy, raw, unboned, real, dead frog" if you want to avoid prosecution.

MR. HILTON

What about our sales?

CONSTABLE

I don't give a damn about your sales. We have to protect the public! Now, what is this one? Number five: "Ram's Bladder Cup!" Now what kind of confectionery is this?

MR. HILTON

We use choice juicy chunks of fresh Cornish ram's bladder, emptied, steamed, flavored with sesame seeds, whipped into a fondue, and garnished with larks' vomit!

CONSTABLE

Larks' vomit?

MR. HILTON

Correct.

CONSTABLE

It doesn't say anything down here about larks' vomit!

MR. HILTON

Ah, yes, it does, on the bottom of the box, after monosodium glutamate.

CONSTABLE

I hardly think this is good enough! It would be more appropriate if the box bore a big red label. "Warning: Larks' Vomit!"

MR. HILTON

Our sales would plummet!

CONSTABLE
Well, why don't you move into more conventional areas of confectionery, like praline or lime cream, a very popular flavor I'm led to understand, or Strawberry Delight? I mean, what's this one? "Cockroach Cluster"? And this, "Anthrax Ripple"?

Constable Parrot vomits into his helmet.

And what's this one, "Spring Surprise"?

MR. HILTON
Aaah, that's our specialty! Covered in darkest, rich, smooth chocolate, when you pop it in your mouth, stainless steel bolts sprint out and punch straight through both cheeks!

CONSTABLE
If people pop a nice chocky in their mouth they don't expect to get their cheeks pierced! In any case, it is an inadequate description of the sweetmeat. I shall have to ask you to accompany me to the station.

MR. HILTON
It's a fair cop.

CONSTABLE
And don't talk to the audience!

Travel Agent

A rather silly man enters and walks up to a young lady at a desk in front of a travel poster which says "Morocco – Sun, Sea, And Watch Out Behind You."

MR. SMOKETOOMUCH

Good morning.

SECRETARY

Oh, good morning. Have you come to arrange a holiday or would you like a blow job?

MR. SMOKETOOMUCH

I'm sorry?

SECRETARY

Oh, you've come to arrange a holiday?

MR. SMOKETOOMUCH

Uuh…yes.

SECRETARY

Oh, sorry, sorry. Now, where were you thinking of going?

MR. SMOKETOOMUCH

To India.

SECRETARY

Ah, one of our *Adventure* holidays eh?

MR. SMOKETOOMUCH

Yes, that's right.

SECRETARY

Well, you'd better see Mr. Bounder about that. Mr. Bounder, this gentleman is interested in the "India Overland" – and *nothing else.*

MR. BOUNDER

Ah. Hello, I'm Bounder of Adventure.

MR. SMOKETOOMUCH

Oh, hello. My name is Smoketoomuch.

MR. BOUNDER

What?

MR. SMOKETOOMUCH

My name is Smoketoomuch. Mr. Smoketoomuch.

MR. BOUNDER

Well, you'd better cut down a little then.

MR. SMOKETOOMUCH

I'm sorry?

MR. BOUNDER

You'd better cut down a little then. (*Laughs*)

MR. SMOKETOOMUCH

Oh, I see! Smoke too much so I'd better cut down a little then!

MR. BOUNDER

Yes. I suppose you get people making jokes about your name all the time, eh?

MR. SMOKETOOMUCH

No, actually, it never struck me before. Smoke-too-much!
(*He laughs uproariously*)

MR. BOUNDER

Anyway, you're interested in one of our Adventure holidays, are you?

MR. SMOKETOOMUCH

Yes, that's right. I saw your advert in the Blassified Ads.

79

MR. BOUNDER

The what?

MR. SMOKETOOMUCH

In The Times Blassified Ads.

MR. BOUNDER

The Times Classified Ads.

MR. SMOKETOOMUCH

Yes, that's right. I'm afraid I have a speech impediment. I can't pronounce the letter B.

MR. BOUNDER

C?

MR. SMOKETOOMUCH

Yes, that's right: B. It's all due to a trauma I suffered when I was a sboolboy. I was attacked by a Siamese bat.

MR. BOUNDER

Ah, a Siamese cat.

MR. SMOKETOOMUCH

No, a Siamese bat. They're more dangerous.

MR. BOUNDER

Listen…can you say the letter K?

MR. SMOKETOOMUCH

Oh, yes. Khaki, Kind, Kettle, Kipling, Kipper, Kuwait, Keble Bollege Oxford, Kellogg's Born Flakes.

MR. BOUNDER

Well, why don't you say the letter K instead of the letter C?

MR. SMOKETOOMUCH

What, you mean, pronounce "blassified" with a K?

MR. BOUNDER

Yes, absolutely!

MR. SMOKETOOMUCH

Classified!

MR. BOUNDER

Good!

MR. SMOKETOOMUCH

Oh, that's very good! I never thought of that before. What a silly bunt.

MR. BOUNDER

Now then, about the holiday…

MR. SMOKETOOMUCH

Yes, well, I've been on package tours many times before, so your advert really bought my eye.

MR. BOUNDER

Good, good, jolly good, well, let me offer you this…

MR. SMOKETOOMUCH

I mean what is the point of going abroad, if you're just another tourist…

MR. BOUNDER

Mmm.

MR. SMOKETOOMUCH

…carted around in buses surrounded by sweaty mindless oafs from Kettering and Coventry…

MR. BOUNDER

Absolutely.

MR. SMOKETOOMUCH

…in their cloth caps and their cardigans and their transistor radios and their *Sunday Mirrors*, complaining about the tea *oh they don't make it properly, do they?* And stopping at endless Majorcan bodegas selling fish and chips and Watneys Red Barrel and calamaris and two veg and sitting in their cotton sun frocks, squirting Timothy White's sun cream all over their puffy, raw, swollen, purulent flesh, cause they overdid it on the first day.

MR. BOUNDER

Yes, I know just what you mean! Now, what we offer is…

MR. SMOKETOOMUCH

And being herded into countless Hotel Miramars and Bellevueses, and Bontinentals with their international luxury modern roomettes…

MR. BOUNDER

Oh, yes.

MR. SMOKETOOMUCH

…and swimming pools full of draft Red Barrel and fat German businessmen pretending to be acrobats and forming pyramids and frightening the children and…

MR. BOUNDER

Oh, yes.

MR. SMOKETOOMUCH

…barging into the queues. And if you're not at your table spot on seven you miss your bowl of Campbell's Cream of Mushroom Soup, the first item on the menu of International Cuisine.

MR. BOUNDER

Absolutely. Now what we have here is…

MR. SMOKETOOMUCH

And every Thursday night there's bloody cabaret in the bar featuring some tiny emaciated dago with nine-inch hips and some fat bloated tart with her hair Brylcreemed down and a big arse presenting flamenco for foreigners.

MR. BOUNDER

Will you be quiet, please?

MR. SMOKETOOMUCH

And adenoidal typists from Birmingham with flabby white legs and diarrhea trying to pick up hairy, bandy-legged Wop waiters called Manuel.

MR. BOUNDER

Will you be quiet?

MR. SMOKETOOMUCH

And once a week there's an excursion to the local Roman remains, where you can buy Cherry Aid and melted ice cream…

MR. BOUNDER

Be quiet!

MR. SMOKETOOMUCH

…and bleedin' Watneys Red Barrel.

MR. BOUNDER

Shut up!

MR. SMOKETOOMUCH

And one night they take you to a typical restaurant with local atmosphere and color and you sit next to a party of people from Torremolinos…

MR. BOUNDER

Shut up!

MR. SMOKETOOMUCH

…who keep singing "I love the Costa Brava!"

MR. BOUNDER

Shut up!

MR. SMOKETOOMUCH

"I love the Costa Brava!"

But Bounder has called for assistance and a gentleman in a white coat leads Smoketoomuch off through the audience still ranting.

And you get cornered by some drunken greengrocer from Luton with an Instamatic camera and last Tuesday's *Daily Express* and he drones on and on and on about how Labour is ruining the country and how many languages Enoch Powell can speak and then he throws up all over the Cuba Libras… And sending tinted postcards of places they don't realize they haven't even visited to "All at number 22, weather wonderful, our room is marked with an 'X', food very greasy but we've found a charming little local place hidden away in the back streets where they serve Watneys Red Barrel and cheese and onion crisps and the accordionist plays 'Maybe its because I'm a Londoner.'" And spending four days on the tarmac at Luton Airport on a five-day package tour with nothing to eat but dry British Airways sandwiches…and you can't even get a glass of Watneys Red Barrel because you're still in England and the bloody bar closes every time you're thirsty. And the kids are crying and vomiting and breaking the plastic ashtrays and they keep telling you it'll only be another hour, but you know damn well your plane is still in Iceland, and has to come back and take a party of Swedes to Yugoslavia before it can come back and load you up at 3 A.M. in the morning. And *then* you sit on the tarmac for four hours because of unforeseen difficulties, i.e. the permanent strike of air traffic control over Paris. And when you finally get to Malaga Airport, everybody's queuing for the bloody toilets and queing for the bloody armed customs officers, and queing for the bloody bus that isn't there, waiting to take you to the hotel that hasn't yet been built. And when you finally get to the half-built Algerian ruin called the Hotel Del Sol by paying half your holiday money to a licensed bandit in a taxi, there's no water in the pool, there's no water in the bath, there's no water in the tap, and there's only a bleeding lizard in the bidet. And half the rooms are double booked, and you can't sleep anyhow, because of the permanent twenty-four-hour sound of them building the hotel next door. Meanwhile, the Spanish National Tourist Board promises you that the raging cholera epidemic is merely a mild outbreak of Spanish Tummy, like the previous outbreak in 1616 which killed half Europe and even the bloody rats are dying from it!

Meanwhile the cast have assembled on stage for…

Custard Pie

A lecturer stands at a lectern. Three men in overalls stand waiting as for a lecture.

LECTURER

As early as the late fourteenth century, or indeed as late as the early fourteenth century, the earliest forms of japes were divisible into…

But Smoketoomuch has escaped his handler and appears in the balcony.

MR. SMOKETOOMUCH

Meanwhile, the bloody Guardia are busy arresting sixteen-year-olds for kissing in the streets and everybody's buying awful horrid little straw donkeys and bullfight posters with their names on, Ordonez, Manito and Mr. Brian Pules of Norwich and when you finally get to Manchester, there's a four-hour wait for another bloody bus to carry you another sixty miles…

But mercifully he is chased off by the white-coated gentleman.

LECTURER

As early as the late fourteenth century – or, indeed, as late as the early fourteenth century, the earliest forms of jape were divisible into the two categories in which I now intend to divide them. As will be seen from the demonstration, the earliest manifestation of the Basic Simple Precipitation Jest incurred a disproportionate amount of internal risibility on the part of the operator.

C takes up middle of stage and sticks out foot in obvious manner.

B walks slowly up to him and falls over foot.

A then forces a very unrealistic grin.

B picks himself up.

Both make slight bowing movement and walk back to centre stage.

This Jest owes its popularity in part, no doubt, to the fact that it may be performed at any time or place by the minimal number of two. There is, however, a variant form involving maximum participation by a group of any size. We may designate this *Secondary* Precipitation.

A and B step forward as if to trip each other and C falls between them.

All face the Audience and then return to their original positions.

Tertiary Precipitation occurs when both protagonists and dupe are located indoors. It is true that this has involved the development of a special piece of machinery.

An assistant holds up a chair, then places it in position.

But it is still no more than a simple variation of Primary or Secondary Precipitation.

A takes his position behind the chair.

B walks across the stage, and turns to sit in the chair as it is snatched away.

He falls painfully.

Both bow to the audience and then return to their original positions.

The opening-up of the African Continent revealed a vast new source of wealth for humorous exploitation.

A banana is brought out and held up.

We are to see demonstrated how this was adapted to the basic precipitation jape.

C walks to the stage left.

B places the banana on centre stage and stands back with anticipated relish.

C walks over banana without falling and finishes his cross to stage right.

B double-takes.

C turns around and walks back to centre stage, looks down at banana peel, picks it up and stuffs banana into the front of B's boiler suit and rubs it around.

C and B bow to audience and return to their positions.

We now come onto a consideration of the more sophisticated Transitive mode of japing, in which as you will observe, the operator or inceptor remains totally unaware of the humorous implications of his action.

A picks up a plank and moves to right of centre with B standing to his left.

A positions the plank on his shoulder.

C stands far stage right.

First we are to see the simple sideswipe or "wop."

C

Hey, Vance!

A turns stage right to C and thus strikes B squarely on the back of his head with the end of the plank as expected.

B falls to the ground but gets up quickly.

Both turn to face the audience again.

LECTURER

Next, the "Sideswipe and Return."

C

Hey, Vance!

This time A turns all the way upstage and in doing so strikes B again on the back of his head with the plank.

A starts to turn back to face audience as B gets up just in time to be hit fully in the face by the plank.

B falls to the ground and takes a long time to get up.

Both turn to face the audience again.

LECTURER

And now, the "Double Sideswipe and Return."

C marches over to stand on A's left facing upstage.

C

Hey, Vance!

A turns to face upstage thus hitting both B and C in the head.

B and C quickly stand up facing the audience only to be hit again by C's plank as C turns back to face the audience.

A, B and C bow to the audience.

The plank is taken off.

LECTURER

Popular as this jest has always been, however, it cannot compare with the ribald connotations associated with the dispatch of an Edible Missile.

A tray containing six custard pies is brought on by Assistant. Each tray has two pies.

First, the "Simple Straightforward Offensive Deposit."

C and B face each other and C deliberately and slowly pushes pie in B's face.

They turn back to the audience.

Second, the "Simple Sideways Offensive Deposit."

A's left hand shoots out and pushes a pie into the side of B's head.

Neither looks away from the audience.

Next, the "Simple Surprise Deposit."

C and B make as if to repeat the action, but before B can throw his pie, C catches him in the face with an under swing. Freeze. Return to the audience.

The "Frustrated Offensive."

B and A turn as each makes to throw a pie at the other but the pies collide.

And now, the "Foul Pie."

A and B turn as each makes to throw a pie but A pushes a pie into the groin of B.

Could we have new pies, please?

The Assistant brings on a tray of four pies.

A and C take two pies each, but B puts his pies down on the tray to wipe his face.

The Assistant leaves before B can re-collect his pies, which he realizes and he double-takes on the fact that he is left without.

Finally we move on to the interesting but little known variant nominally designated the "Three-Course Complex."

B and A face each other and C faces the back of B.

A makes to throw his pie at B.

B ducks and his pie hits C.

B stands up pleased, by which time C has made to throw at A, thereby catching B in the back of his head.

Immediately A makes to throw again but this time holds on to it, and as B ducks, A pushes his pie safely into the back of B's head as he ducks, and at that same time C has leant forward and thrust his last pie into a low position, so that when B ducks he automatically ducks into C's pie.

A, B and C all freeze momentarily and then return to positions.

But finally, we must not forget the enjoyment, satisfaction, amusement and the edification to be derived from the "Simple Straightforward Sideways Completely Unexpected Deposit."

As the Lecturer is speaking, another man in a white lab coat creeps up behind the Lecturer with a chair and a pie. The Intruder mounts his chair, winds up and is about to pie the Lecturer in the face but at the last minute the Lecturer produces a pie and pies the Intruder.

– Curtain –

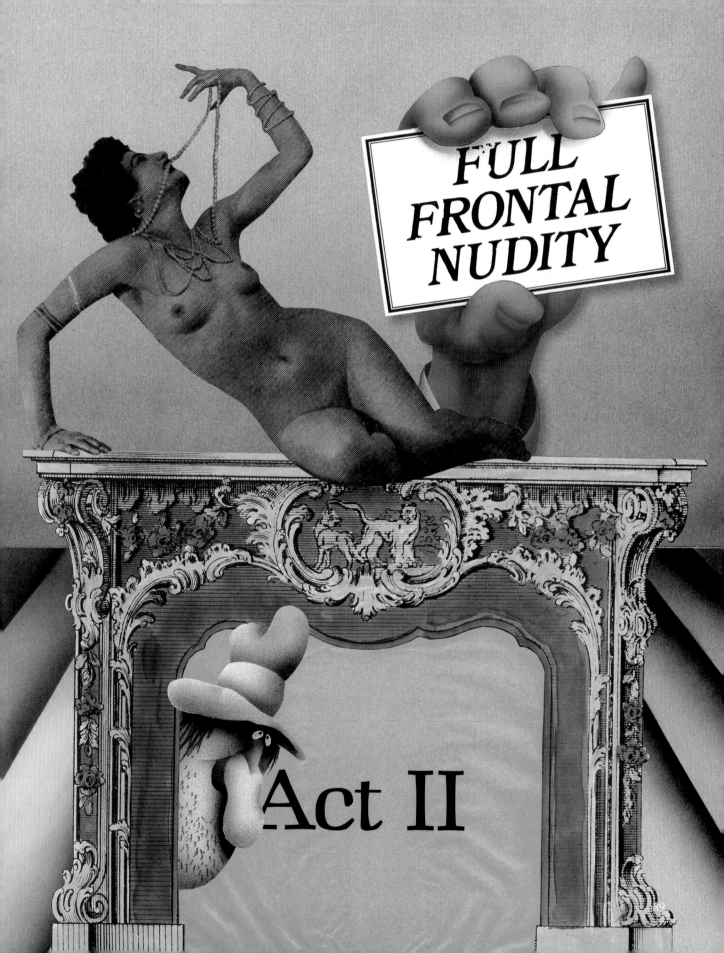

FULL
FRONTAL
NUDITY

Act II

Sit on My Face

Four elegantly dressed French waiters in waistcoats and long white pinafores sing.

Sit on my face, and tell me that you love me
I'll sit on your face and tell you I love you, too.
I love to hear you oralize
When I'm between your thighs
You blow me away.

Sit on my face and let my lips embrace you
I'll sit on your face and then you'll love me truly.
Life can be fine if we both 69
If we sit on our faces in all kinds of places and play
Till we're blown away!

The waiters bow, turn and walk off revealing they have bare bottoms.

90

Camp Judges

Two Judges in full wigs and red robes enter and walk to a coat stand in centre stage.

BARRISTER I

(taking his wig off and shaking his hair out)

Ooh, I had a bitch of a morning in the High Court! I could stamp my little feet at the way those counsels carry on.

BARRISTER II

Oh, don't tell me, love.

BARRISTER I

Objection here, objection there, and that nice policeman giving his evidence so well! Beautiful speaking voice.

BARRISTER II

And what a body!

BARRISTER I

Oh, yeah. Well, after a bit all I could do was bang me gavel.

BARRISTER II

You what, love?

BARRISTER I

I banged me gavel!

BARRISTER II

Oh, get away!

BARRISTER I

I did! I did my "silence in court" bit.

BARRISTER II

Ooh.

BARRISTER I

If looks could have killed, that prosecuting counsel would have been in for thirty years. How did your summing-up go?

Removes his robe to reveal a shimmering body stocking and garter belt underneath.

BARRISTER II

Well, I was trying it in me butch voice: you know, "What the jury must understand," and you know they loved it!

BARRISTER I

I bet they did.

BARRISTER II

I could see that little curly-headed foreman of the jury eyeing me!

BARRISTER I

Really?

BARRISTER II

Oh, yeah. Cheeky devil. I got really strict. I finished up with: "the actions of these vicious men are a violent stain on the community and the full penalty of the law is scarcely sufficient to deal with their ghastly crimes!"

Removes his final garment to reveal a French bustier and black stockings.

BARRISTER I

Oh, yeah?

BARRISTER II

And I waggled me wig!

BARRISTER I
You waggled your what?

BARRISTER II
I waggled me wig!

BARRISTER I
Really?

BARRISTER II
Ever so slightly, stunning effect.

BARRISTER I
Ooh!

BARRISTER II
Anyway, I gave him three years. It only took ten minutes…

BARRISTER II
Well, as I said the other day, you know: "You can put it in the hand of your attorneys, but it'll never stand up in court!"

As they walk off arm in arm.

Albatross

A large man in drag appears as an ice cream saleslady holding a confectionery tray with a large albatross on it.

WOMAN

Albatross! Albatross! Albatross!
Seagull sickle! Pelican-bonbon! Stormy Petrel on a stick. Albatross!

A City Gent with a bowler hat and moustache approaches.

MAN

Could I have two ice creams, please?

WOMAN

I haven't got any ice creams, I just got this albatross! Albatross!

MAN

What flavor is it?

WOMAN

Well, it is an albatross, isn't it? There's no bloody flavor! Albatross!

MAN

There's gotta be some flavor, I mean everything's got a flavor…

WOMAN

All right, all right! It's bloody albatross flavor!
Bleedin' seabird, bleedin' flavor! Albatross!

MAN

Do you get wafers with it?

WOMAN

Of course you don't get fucking wafers with it, it's a fucking albatross.

Enter a Colonel.

COLONEL

Right stop that! Stop that! It's filthy! Now no one enjoys a good laugh more
than I do. Except perhaps for my wife and some of her friends.
Oh, yes, and Captain Johnson. Come to think of it, most
people enjoy a good laugh more than I do, but that's
beside the point. You're not even a proper woman!

WOMAN

Don't you oppress me, mate!

COLONEL

Get off!

WOMAN

Bleedin' sexist!

COLONEL

Right! Let's get on with this skit!
And…cue…the…skit!

Nudge Nudge

NORMAN

Evening, squire!

MAN

Good evening.

NORMAN

Is your wife a…goer? Eh? Know what I mean? Know what I mean?
Nudge, nudge! Know what I mean? Say no more!

MAN

I beg your pardon?

NORMAN

Your wife…does she "go" eh? Know what I mean? Does she "go"? Eh?

MAN

She sometimes has to go.

NORMAN

I bet she does! I bet she does! Say no more! Say no more!
Know what I mean? Nudge, nudge!

MAN

I'm afraid I don't quite follow you…

NORMAN

Oh, "follow me, follow me"? Very good, that's very good!
A nod's as good as a wink to a blind bat!

MAN

Are you selling something?

NORMAN

"Selling, selling"...very good indeed!
You're wicked, you are, eh?
Wicked, eh? Whoa! Wicked! *Say no more!*

MAN

What?

NORMAN

Is your wife interested in *sport*? Eh?

MAN

She likes sport, yes.

NORMAN

I bet she does! I bet she does!

MAN

As a matter of fact, she's very fond of cricket.

NORMAN

She likes "games," eh? Likes "games"?
Knew she would, she's been around a bit, eh? She's been around?

MAN

Well, she has traveled, yes. She's from Purley.

NORMAN

Oh *say* no more! Purley, squire? Say no more! Say no more!
Say no more! Say no more!

MAN

Well...

NORMAN

And is your wife interested in...photography? Eh? Eh? Eh?

MAN

Photography?

NORMAN

"Photographs, eh?" He asked him knowingly!

MAN

Photography?

NORMAN

Snap, snap, grin, grin, wink, wink, nudge, nudge, say no more!

MAN

Holiday snaps?

NORMAN

They could be, they could be taken on holiday.
Swimming costumes, you know, candid "candid" photography?

MAN

No, we don't have a camera!

NORMAN

Oh. Still, whoahaah! Eh? (*Rude hand gesture repeated*) Whoahaah! Eh? Whoahaah! Eh? Whoahaahaha!

MAN

Look, are you insinuating something?

NORMAN

Oh, no, no, no…yes!

MAN

Well?

NORMAN

Well, I mean, you're a man of the world, squire, you know…you've been around, you know, you've been around a bit?

MAN

What do you mean?

NORMAN

Well, I mean, like, you know you've…done it, you've slept…with a lady?

MAN

Yes.

NORMAN

What's it like?

– Blackout –

Pepperpots

Two elderly ladies.

PP2

Hallo, Mrs. Thing.

PP1

Hallo, Mrs. Entity…

PP2

How are you then?

PP1

Oh I've had a morning.

PP2

Busy?

PP1

Busy! I got up at five o'clock, made myself a cup of tea, looked out the window, well by then I was so worn out I had to come and have a sit down. I've been here seven hours.

PP2

You must be exhausted

PP1

Have you been shopping?

PP2

No. I've been shopping.

PP1

Funny.

PP2

I'm worn out. Six hours I've been shopping.

PP1

What have you bought?

PP2

Nothing. Nothing at all. A complete waste of time.

PP1

Wicked isn't it?

PP2

Wicked. And it'll be worse when we join the Common Market.

PP1

That nice Mr. Heath would never allow it.

PP2

Funny he never married.

99

PP1

He's a bachelor.

PP2

Ooh! That would explain it. Oh dear me this chatting away wears me out.

PP1

I bet Mrs. Reginald Maudling doesn't have to put up with this drudgery, getting up in the morning, making tea, looking out of the window, chatting away.

PP2

No! It'd all be done for her.

PP1

Yes, I expect she's got the whole day free for playing snooker.

PP2

She wouldn't go through all the drudgery of playing snooker day in and day out.

PP1

No, it'd all be done for her. She wouldn't need to lift a cue.

PP2

She probably doesn't even know where the billiard room is.

PP1

Not like the old days. Mrs. Stanley Baldwin had to get up at five o'clock, go out and catch partridges with her bare hands.

PP2

Yes…and Mrs. William Pitt the Elder had to get up at three o'clock and burrow for truffles with the bridge of her nose.

PP1

Mrs. Beethoven had to get up at midnight to spur on the mynah bird.

PP2

Lazy creatures mynah birds.

PP1

Yes, after Beethoven went deaf the mynah bird just used to mime.

PP2

Ooh! What's happening?

PP1

Don't worry it's only a flashback.

PP2

Ooh!

International Philosophy

GERMANY vs. GREECE

A football stadium.

VOICE-OVER

Good afternoon, and welcome to a packed Olympic stadium in Munich for the second leg of this exciting final. And here come the Germans now, led out by their skipper "Nobby" Hegel. They must truly be favorites this afternoon. They've certainly attracted the most attention from the press with their team problems. And let's now see their line-up:

DEUTSCHLAND

1 LEIBNIZ
2 I. KANT
3 HEGEL
4 SCHOPENHAUER
5 SCHELLING
6 BECKENBAUER
7 JASPERS
8 SCHLEGEL
9 WITTGENSTEIN
10 NIETZSCHE
11 HEIDEGGER

VOICE-OVER

The Germans playing 4–2–4, Leibniz in goal, back four Kant, Hegel, Schopenhauer, and Schelling, front runners Schlegel, Wittgenstein, Nietzsche, and Heidegger, and the midfield duo of Beckenbauer and Jaspers. Beckenbauer obviously a bit of a surprise there. And here come the Greeks, led out by their veteran center-half Heraclitus. Let's look at their team…

GREECE

1 PLATO
2 EPICTETUS
3 ARISTOTLE
4 SOPHOCLES
5 EMPEDOCLES OF ACRAGAS
6 PLOTINUS
7 EPICURUS
8 HERACLITUS
9 DERACLITUS
10 SOCRATES
11 ARCHIMEDES

VOICE-OVER

And as expected it's a much more defensive line-up. Plato's in goal, Socrates is a front runner there, and Aristotle as sweeper. Aristotle, very much the man in form. One surprise is the inclusion of Archimedes. Well, here comes the referee Confucius and his two linesmen, St. Augustine and St. Thomas Aquinas. And as the two skippers come together to shake hands we're ready for the start of this very exciting final. The referee, Mr. Confucius, checks his sand…

Referee's whistle.

VOICE-OVER

…and…they're off!

Nothing happens. The Philosophers ignore the football and wander around philosophizing.

VOICE-OVER

Nietzsche and Hegel there, Karl Jaspers on the outside, Wittgenstein there with him, there's Beckenbauer, Schelling there, Heidegger covering, Schopenhauer, and now it's the Greeks. Epicurus, number six, Aristotle, Empedocles and Deraclitus, and Heraclitus with him, there's Archimedes, Socrates, there he is, Socrates, Socrates there going through… and there's the ball. Well we'll be bringing you back to this exciting contest the moment anything interesting happens.

GERMANY 0   GREECE 0

Never Be Rude to an Arab

(A Plea for Understanding in a Troubled World)

A Gentleman in white tie and tails stands next to a potted plant and sings.

GENTLEMAN

Never be rude to an Arab
An Israeli or Saudi or Jew
Never be rude to an Irishman
No matter what you do!

Never poke fun at a nigger
A Spik or a Wop or a Kraut
And never poke fun at a Pollack…

*The potted plant beside
him explodes.*

103

International Philosophy Part 2

VOICE-OVER

Welcome back. Well, there may be no score, but there's certainly no lack of excitement here, as you can see, Nietzsche has just been booked for arguing with the referee. He accused Confucius of having no free will, and Confucius he say name go in book, and this is Nietzsche's third booking in four games. Oh and that is Karl Marx. Karl Marx is warming up, it looks as if there is going to be a substitution on the German side. Obviously manager Martin Luther has decided on all-out attack and indeed he must, with only two minutes of the match to go. But the big question is: Who is going to be replaced? Who is going to come off? It could be Jaspers, Hegel or Schopenhauer. But it's Wittgenstein! Wittgenstein who only last week had his name in the blue book…

And so here's Marx! Let's see if he can put some fight into this German attack…

Karl Marx runs on very determinedly. Then begins to philosophize and walk around ignoring the ball like the others.

Evidently not. What a shame. Well, now, with just over a minute left, a replay of Tuesday looks absolutely inevitable. There's Archimedes, and I think he's had an idea!

Archimedes has an idea.

ARCHIMEDES

Eureka!

Archimedes runs over and kicks the ball. He starts off a beautiful flowing attacking move by the Grecian team, who run rings around the Germans.

VOICE-OVER

Archimedes out to Socrates, Socrates back to Archimedes, Archimedes out to Heraclitus, he beats Hegel, Heraclitus a little flick, here comes the cross: Socrates, Socrates is there! It's in! Goooooaal! The Greeks are going mad! The Greeks on the replay there and Socrates scores with a beautiful header.   But the Germans are disputing it! Hegel is arguing that reality is merely an a-priori by-product of contemporary ethics, Kant by the Categorical Imperative is holding that ontologically it exists only in the imagination and Marx is claiming it was off-side! But Confucius blows the final whistle…it's all over! Germany, having trounced England's famous midfield trio of Bentham, Locke and Hobbes in the semifinal, have been beaten by the odd goal! And there it is again, in slow mo, Socrates, Socrates heads it in, and Leibniz just has no chance! And just look at those delighted Greeks! There they are, Chopper Socrates, Empedocles, and Deraclitus! What a game here! And Epicurus is there, and Socrates, the captain who scored what must probably be the most important goal of his career!

Argument

SECRETARY
Good afternoon, sir. May I help you?

CUSTOMER
Yes, I'd like to have an argument, please.

SECRETARY
Certainly, sir. Have you been here before?

CUSTOMER
Ah, no, this is my first time.

SECRETARY
I see. Well, do you want to have just one argument or were you thinking of taking a course?

CUSTOMER
Well, what is the cost?

SECRETARY
It's one pound for a five-minute argument, but only eight pounds for a course of ten.

CUSTOMER
Well, I think I'll just try the one and see how it goes from there.

SECRETARY
Fine. Ah, yes, try Mr. Barnard, Room 12.

CUSTOMER
Thank you very much.

The Customer enters a room.

MR. BARNARD

(*aggressively*)

What do you want?

CUSTOMER

Well, I was just…

MR. BARNARD

Don't give me that! You snotty-faced heap of parrot droppings! Shut your festering gob, you tit! Your type make me puke, you vacuous, stuffy, old malodorous pervert!

CUSTOMER

Listen, I came here for an argument!

MR. BARNARD

Oh, I'm sorry. This is Abuse.

CUSTOMER

Oh, I see!

MR. BARNARD

Hahaha!

CUSTOMER

Terribly sorry.

MR. BARNARD

No, you want Room 12A, next door.

CUSTOMER

I see. Thank you very much.

MR. BARNARD

Not at all. Stupid git.

The Customer moves on.

CUSTOMER

Is this the right room for an argument?

ARGUER

I told you once.

CUSTOMER

No, you haven't.

ARGUER

Yes, I have.

CUSTOMER

When?

ARGUER

Just now.

CUSTOMER

No, you didn't.

ARGUER

Yes, I did.

CUSTOMER

You didn't.

ARGUER

I did.

CUSTOMER

No, you didn't!

ARGUER

I'm telling you I did.

CUSTOMER

You most certainly did not!

ARGUER

Ah, wait a moment, is this the five-minute argument or the full half hour?

CUSTOMER

Oh. Oh I see. It's just the five-minute.

ARGUER

Just the five minutes. *(Writing)* Right, thank you. Anyway, I did.

CUSTOMER

Oh no you didn't.

ARGUER

Now let's get one thing absolutely clear. I most definitely told you.

CUSTOMER

No, you didn't.

ARGUER

Yes, I did.

CUSTOMER

No, you didn't.

ARGUER

Yes, I did.

CUSTOMER

No, you didn't.

ARGUER

Yes, I did.

CUSTOMER

No, you didn't.

ARGUER

Yes, I did.

CUSTOMER

No, you didn't.

ARGUER

Yes, I did.

CUSTOMER

No, you didn't.

ARGUER

Yes, I did.

CUSTOMER

No, you didn't.

ARGUER

Yes, I did.

CUSTOMER

No, you didn't.

ARGUER

Yes, I did.

CUSTOMER

No, you didn't.

ARGUER

Yes, I did.

CUSTOMER

No, you didn't.

ARGUER

Yes, I did.

CUSTOMER

Oh, look, this isn't an argument!

ARGUER

Yes, it is!

CUSTOMER

No, it isn't! It's just contradiction!

ARGUER

No, it isn't!

CUSTOMER

It is!

ARGUER

It is not!

CUSTOMER

It is! You just contradicted me!

ARGUER

I did not!

CUSTOMER

You did!

ARGUER

No, no, no!

CUSTOMER

You did just then!

ARGUER

Nonsense!

CUSTOMER

Oh, this is futile!

ARGUER

No, it isn't.

CUSTOMER

Yes, it is. I came here for a good argument.

ARGUER

No, you didn't. You came here for an argument.

CUSTOMER

Yes, but an argument isn't just contradiction!

ARGUER

Well, it can be.

CUSTOMER

No. An argument is a connected series of
statements intended to establish a proposition.

ARGUER

No, it isn't!

CUSTOMER

Yes, it is! It isn't just contradiction!

ARGUER

Look, if I argue with you, I must take a contrary position.

CUSTOMER

Yes, but that isn't just saying "No, it isn't!"

ARGUER

Yes, it is!

CUSTOMER

No, it isn't!

ARGUER

Yes, it is!

CUSTOMER

No, it isn't!

ARGUER

Yes, it is!

CUSTOMER

No, it isn't!

ARGUER

Yes, it is!

CUSTOMER

No, it isn't!

ARGUER

Yes, it is!

CUSTOMER

Argument is an intellectual process. Contradiction
is just an automatic gainsaying of anything the other person says!

ARGUER

It is not!

CUSTOMER

It is!

ARGUER

Not at all!

CUSTOMER

Now look…

The Arguer slams his hand down on a little bell.

ARGUER

Thank you! Good morning!

CUSTOMER

What?

ARGUER

That's it! Good morning!

CUSTOMER

I was just getting interested!

ARGUER

I'm sorry, the five minutes is up!

CUSTOMER

That was never five minutes, just now!

ARGUER

I'm afraid it was.

CUSTOMER

Oh no it wasn't.

ARGUER

I'm sorry, I'm not allowed to argue anymore.

CUSTOMER

What?

ARGUER

If you want me to go on arguing, you'll have to pay for another five minutes.

CUSTOMER

But that was never five minutes, just now!

The Arguer ignores him, whistling tunelessly.

Oh, come on! Oh, this is ridiculous!

ARGUER

If you want me to go on arguing, you'll have to pay for another five minutes!

CUSTOMER

Oh, all right. Here you are.

Customer hands over cash which the Arguer pockets.

ARGUER

Thank you.

CUSTOMER

Well?

ARGUER

Well what?

CUSTOMER

That was never five minutes, just now!

ARGUER

I told you, if you want me to go on arguing, you'll have to pay for another five minutes.

CUSTOMER

I've just paid!

ARGUER

No, you didn't!

CUSTOMER

I did!

ARGUER

You did not!

CUSTOMER

I did!

ARGUER

You never…

CUSTOMER

I did!

ARGUER

You never…

CUSTOMER

I did!

ARGUER

You never…

CUSTOMER

Look I don't want to argue about that.

ARGUER

Well, I'm very sorry, but you didn't pay!

CUSTOMER

Aha! But if I didn't pay, why are you arguing? Ahaaa! Got you!

ARGUER

No, you haven't.

CUSTOMER

Yes, I have. If you're arguing, I must have paid.

ARGUER

Not necessarily. I could be arguing in my spare time.

CUSTOMER

Oh, I've had enough of this!

ARGUER

No, you haven't!

CUSTOMER

Yes, I have!

ARGUER

No, you haven't!

CUSTOMER

Yes, I have!

ARGUER

No, you haven't!

CUSTOMER

Oh shut up!

A Strange Man descends from the ceiling and sings to a small ukulele.

I've Got Two Legs

STRANGE MAN

I've got two legs from my hips to the ground
And when I lift them they walk around
And when I lift them they climb the stairs
And when I shave them they ain't got hairs

The Arguer picks up a rifle and shoots him and his belly explodes.

STRANGE MAN

Arrggghhhh!

Four Yorkshiremen

Four men in white tuxedos and wih cigars sit at a table centre stage. One pours wine into glasses.

HEZEKIAH

Very passable, isn't it?

ALL

Very passable.

OBADIAH

Good glass of Château de Chasselay, ain't that, so Josiah?

JOSIAH

Oh, you're right there, Obadiah.

OBADIAH

Right.

EZEKIEL

Who would have thought, thirty years ago, we'd all be sitting here drinking Château de Chasselay eh? eh?

ALL

Aye, aye.

HEZEKIAH

In them days we were glad to have the price of a cup of tea.

OBADIAH

A cup of *cold* tea!

HEZEKIAH

Right!

EZEKIEL

Without milk or sugar!

JOSIAH

Or tea!

HEZEKIAH

In a cracked cup and all.

EZEKIEL

Oh, we never used to have a cup! We used to have to drink out of a rolled-up newspaper!

OBADIAH

The best we could manage was to suck on a piece of damp cloth.

JOSIAH

But you know, we were happy in those days, although we were poor.

HEZEKIAH

Because we were poor!

JOSIAH

Right!

HEZEKIAH

My old dad used to say to me: "Money doesn't buy you happiness, son!"

EZEKIEL

He was right!

HEZEKIAH

Right!

EZEKIEL

I was happier then and I had nothing! We used to live in this tiny old tumbled-down house with great big holes in the roof.

OBADIAH

A house? You were lucky to live in a house! We used to live in one room, all twenty-six of us, no furniture, half the floor was missing, we were all huddled together in one corner for fear of falling.

JOSIAH

You were lucky to have a room! We used to have to live in the corridor!

HEZEKIAH

Oh, we used to dream of living in a corridor! Would have been a palace to us! We used to live in an old water tank on a rubbish tip. We'd all be woke up every morning by having a load of rotting fish dumped all over us! House, huh!

EZEKIEL

Well, when I say a house, it was just a hole in the ground, covered by a sheet of tarpaulin, but it was a house to us!

OBADIAH

We were evicted from our hole in the ground. We had to go and live in a lake!

JOSIAH

You were lucky to have a lake! There were 150 of us living in a shoebox in the middle of the road!

HEZEKIAH

A cardboard box?

JOSIAH

Aye!

HEZEKIAH

You were lucky! We lived for three months in a rolled-up newspaper in a septic tank! We used to have to go up every morning at six o'clock and clean the newspaper, go to work down the mill, fourteen hours a day, week in, week out, for six pence a week, and when we got home, our dad would thrash us to sleep with his belt!

OBADIAH

Luxury! We used to have to get up out of the lake at three o'clock in the morning, clean the lake, eat a handful of hot gravel, work twenty hours a day at mill, for two pence a month, come home, and Dad would beat us around the head and neck with a broken bottle, if we were lucky!

JOSIAH

Well, we had it tough! We used to have to get up out of the shoebox in the middle of the night and lick the road clean with our tongues! We had to eat half a handful of freezing cold gravel, work twenty-four hours a day at mill for four pence every six years, and when we got home, our dad would slice us in two with a bread knife!

EZEKIEL

Right! I had to get up in the morning, at ten o'clock at night, half an hour before I went to bed, eat a lump of cold poison, work twenty-nine hours a day down mill and pay mill owner for permission to come to work, and when we got home, our dad would kill us and dance about on our graves, singing Hallelujah!

HEZEKIAH

Aye. And you trying to tell the young people of today that, and they won't believe you!

ALL

No, no they won't!

– Blackout –

Fairy Tale

STORYTELLER

Once upon a time there was a little house in a dark forest. In this house lived a humble woodcutter and his wife and their pretty daughter, Little Red Riding Hood. And in the middle of this deep, dark forest, there lived a vicious wolf! One day Little Red Riding Hood set off to take some things to her old grandmother who lived deep in the forest. The vicious wolf saw Little Red Riding Hood and thought: She looks very good to eat!

"Where are you going my, pretty one?"

"Oh, kind sir, to my grandmother's."

"Ha, ha, ha, ha!" smirked the wicked wolf and dashed off through the forest to Grandmother's house.

"Knock, knock, knock," went the wicked wolf.

The door opened wide, but it wasn't Grandmother who opened it. It was Buzz Aldrin, America's #2 spaceman! For this was not Granny's little house at all, but the headquarter of NASA, the American space research agency. The wicked wolf was shot by security guards.

So all was quiet in the forest again. The humble woodcutter and his wife sold their story to *Der Spiegel* for forty thousand Deutschmarks. NASA agreed to limit the number of nuclear tests in Granny's little house to two on Thursdays and one on Saturdays after tea.

Parrot

A pet shop.
A Shopkeeper enters. A counter slides across on wheels to meet him.
Mr. Praline enters carrying a dead parrot in a cage.
He walks to the counter, where the shopkeeper tries to hide below a cash register.

PRALINE

I wish to register a complaint. Hello? Miss?

SHOPKEEPER

(*rising*)

What do you mean, Miss?

PRALINE

Oh, I'm sorry. I have a cold. I wish to make a complaint.

SHOPKEEPER

We're closing for lunch.

PRALINE

Never mind that, my lad, I wish to complain about this parrot that
I purchased not half an hour ago from this very boutique.

SHOPKEEPER

Oh yes, the Norwegian blue. What's wrong with it?

PRALINE

I'll tell you what's wrong with it, my lad. It's dead that's what's wrong with it.

SHOPKEEPER

No, no, it's resting, look!

PRALINE

Look my lad, I know a dead parrot when
I see one and I'm looking at one right now.

SHOPKEEPER

No. He's not dead. He's resting.

PRALINE

Resting?

SHOPKEEPER

Yeah, resting. Exceptional bird the Norwegian
blue, beautiful plumage.

PRALINE

The plumage don't enter into it. It's stone dead.

SHOPKEEPER

It's resting.

PRALINE

All right then, if it's resting I'll wake it up. (*Shouts into cage*) Wake up, Polly,
wake up, Polly Parrot. I've got a nice cuttlefish for you, if you wake up, Polly.

SHOPKEEPER

(jogging the cage)

There he moved.

PRALINE

No he didn't. That was you pushing the cage.

SHOPKEEPER

I didn't!

PRALINE

Yes, you did. (*Taking the parrot out of the cage*) Polly, Polly. (*Bangs it against the counter*) Wake up, Polly, wake up. This is your 9 A.M. alarm call. (*Throws the bird in the air and lets it fall to the floor*) Now that's what I call a dead parrot.

SHOPKEEPER

Well it's stunned.

PRALINE

What?

SHOPKEEPER

You stunned it just as it was waking up.

PRALINE

Look my lad, I've had enough of this. That parrot is definitely deceased. And when I bought it not half an hour ago, you assured me that its total lack of movement was due to it being tired and shagged out after a long squawk.

SHOPKEEPER

Well it may be pining for the fjords.

PRALINE

Pining for the fjords? What kind of talk is that? Look, why did it fall flat on its back the moment I got it home?

SHOPKEEPER

The Norwegian blue prefers kipping on it's back! Beautiful bird, lovely plumage!

PRALINE

Look, matey, I took the liberty of examining that parrot, and I discovered the only reason that it had been sitting on its perch in the first place was that it had been nailed there.

SHOPKEEPER

Well of course it was nailed there. Otherwise it would have been through those bars like a flash of lightning.

PRALINE

Look. Those bars are only half an inch apart.

SHOPKEEPER

The Norwegian blue is not only as strong as an ox, it's also extremely adept at fasting. If I hadn't nailed it down it would have muscled up to those bars and voom.

120

PRALINE

Look, my lad. (*Picks up the parrot*) This parrot wouldn't voom if you put four thousand volts through it! It's bleedin' demised!

SHOPKEEPER

It's not, it's pining!

PRALINE

It's not pining, it's passed on. This parrot is no more! It's ceased to be. It's expired and gone to meet its maker. This is a late parrot. It's a stiff. Bereft of life, it rests in peace. It would be pushing up the daisies if you hadn't nailed it to the perch. It's rung down the curtain and joined the choir invisible. This is an ex-parrot.

SHOPKEEPER

Well, I'd better replace it, then.

Shopkeeper exits.

PRALINE

If you want to get anything done in this country you've got to complain till you're blue in the mouth.

Shopkeeper returns.

SHOPKEEPER

Sorry, squire, I've had a look and we're right out of parrots.

PRALINE

I see, I see.

SHOPKEEPER

(Beat.)

I got a slug.

PRALINE

Does it talk?

SHOPKEEPER

Not really, no.

PRALINE

Then it's not much of a bleedin' replacement is it?

Beat.

SHOPKEEPER

D'you want to come back to my place?

Very long beat.

PRALINE

Yeah, all right.

Salvation Fuzz

A Husband and his ratbag Wife are at a table listening to the radio.

RADIO VOICE

(*on slight distort*)

> I think all right-thinking people in this country are sick and tired of being told that ordinary decent people are fed up in this country.

WIFE

(*switching off the radio*)

> Liberal rubbish! What do you want with your jugged fish, Klaus?

HUSBAND

> Pardon, my wide-thighed plum?

WIFE

> What do you want with your jugged fish, you cloth-eared git?

HUSBAND

> Halibut!

WIFE

> The jugged fish is halibut!

HUSBAND

> All right. What fish do you have that is not jugged?

WIFE

> Uuh, rabbit.

HUSBAND

> What, rabbit fish?

WIFE

> Well, it's all covered in fur.

HUSBAND

Is it dead?

WIFE

Well, it was coughing up blood last night.

HUSBAND

All right, I'll have the dead, unjugged rabbit fish.

FEMALE VOICE

One dead, unjugged rabbit fish later.

HUSBAND

Appalling!

WIFE

Oh, you're always complaining.

HUSBAND

What's for afterwards?

WIFE

Well, there's rat pie, rat pudding, rat sorbet or strawberry tart.

HUSBAND

Strawberry tart?

WIFE

Well, it's got some rat in it.

HUSBAND

How much?

WIFE

Six. Rather a lot really.

HUSBAND

I'll have a slice without so much rat in it.

FEMALE VOICE

One slice of strawberry tart without so much rat in it later.

HUSBAND

Appalling!

WIFE

Moan, moan, moan!

SON

Hello, Mom! Hello, Dad!

HUSBAND

Hello, son!

SON

There's a dead bishop on the landing!

WIFE

Where he from?

SON

What do you mean?

WIFE

What's his diocese?

SON

Well, he looked a bit Canterburyish to me.

HUSBAND

I'll go and have a look.

WIFE

I don't know who keeps bringing them in here.

SON

Well, it's not me.

WIFE

I put three out by the trash cans last week and the garbage men won't touch them.

HUSBAND

It's the Bishop of Leicester!

WIFE

How do you know?

HUSBAND

Tattooed on the back of his neck! I think I'd better call the police!

WIFE

Shouldn't you call the church?

SON

Call the church police!

HUSBAND

That's a good idea! (*Shouts*) The church police!

Enter a church policeman.

POLICEMAN

Hello! Hello! Hello. What's all this then? Amen!

WIFE

Are you the church police?

POLICEMAN

Oh, yes!

WIFE

There's another dead bishop on the landing, Sergeant!

POLICEMAN

Detective superintendent, madam! What is he? RC or C of E?

WIFE

How should I know?

POLICEMAN

Tattooed on the back of their neck! Here, is that rat tart?

WIFE

Oh, uh, yes.

POLICEMAN

Disgusting! Right, men! The hunt is on! Let us kneel in prayer!
Oh Lord, we beseech thee. Tell us who croaked the bishop of Leicester.

Thunder. Angels' Choir chants and a finger descends and points.

GOD

The one in the braces, he done it.

HUSBAND

It's a fair cop, but society is to blame.

POLICEMAN

Agreed. We'll arrest them instead! Right, we'd like to conclude this arrest
with a hymn.

All thing's bright and beautiful, all creatures great and small.
All thing's bright and wonderful…

The Husband steps forward and addresses the audience,

HUSBAND

I never wanted to be in such a shambledy sketch. I always wanted to be…
a lumberjack!

The Lumberjack Song

LUMBERJACK

Leaping from tree to tree…as they float down the mighty rivers of British Columbia! The larch…the redwood…the mighty sequioa…The giant deadwood, the spruce…the little Californian rude tree!

A chorus of Mounties appear going Tra La.

With my best girl by my side!

His best Girl runs out beside him.

We'd sing, sing, sing!

LUMBERJACK

Oh I'm a lumberjack and I'm okay,
I sleep all night and I work all day.

CHOIR AND GIRL

He's a lumberjack and he's okay,
He sleeps all night and he works all day.

LUMBERJACK

I cut down trees, I eat my lunch,
I go to the lavatory.
On Wednesdays I go shopping,
And have buttered scones for tea.

CHOIR

He cuts down trees, he eats his lunch,
He goes to the lavatory.
On Wednesdays he goes shopping,
And has buttered scones for tea.

LUMBERJACK

I'm a lumberjack and I'm okay,
I sleep all night and I work all day.

CHOIR AND GIRL

He's a lumberjack and he's okay,
He sleeps all night and he works all day.

LUMBERJACK

I cut down trees, I skip and jump,
I like to press wild flowers.
I put on women's clothing,
And hang around in bars.

CHOIR

He cuts down trees, he skips and jumps,
He likes to press wild flowers.
He puts on women's clothing,
And *hangs around in bars…?*

LUMBERJACK

I'm a lumberjack and I'm okay,
I sleep all night and I work all day.

CHOIR AND GIRL

He's a lumberjack and he's okay,
He sleeps all night and he works all day.

LUMBERJACK

I cut down trees, I wear high heels,
Suspenders and a bra.
I wish I'd been a girlie,
Just like my dear papa.

CHOIR

He cuts down trees, he wears high heels,
Suspenders and a bra?

Song breaks down.

AD-LIB

What kind of god damn fairy faggot…?

They begin to exit.

GIRL

Oh, Bevis, and I thought you were so rugged.

The music begins again and they all come scampering back.

ALL

I'm/He's a lumberjack and I'm okay,
I sleep all night and I work all day.
I'm a lumberjack and I'm okaaaaayyyyy…

An incredibly long note sustained by all forever.

He sleeps all night and he works all day!

Music: Liberty Bell.

On screen: Piss Off!

– Curtain –

In Their Own Words

the Pythons Recall the Touring Years

SO MUCH FOR HISTORY

JOHN CLEESE: What I Remember

What was extraordinary about the Python stage show was the blithe self-confidence with which we embarked on it. Why we were so sure the material would work on stage, I have no idea. But as we always cared more about making each other laugh than about the impact that our jokes would make on strangers, we must have created a protective bubble around us which insulated us from the reality of our situation. From the start, my main concern was to rid myself of the obligation to perform the "Silly Walk" sketch every night. I never rated the sketch highly (it was written by Palin and Jones), but the others absolutely insisted that it should be in the lineup for the first night.

So when, on the first night, I found myself performing it to complete silence, I was relieved. As I cavorted around the Southampton stage, the audience watched, at first apathetically, and then with outright hostility. I felt humiliated, of course, but I was more than compensated by the knowledge that I was performing the last rites on this cheesy bit of material. When I got off stage I announced "Well that's the end of 'Silly Walks.' Good riddance!" But…the others insisted that I give the damn thing one more outing. "Just one," I agreed, "but if it doesn't work tomorrow…" A deal was struck. Sadly, the Brighton audience, morons that they were (compared with the charming and highly sophisticated Southampton mob) started to laugh. Bastards! I experienced a sinking feeling as the chuckles grew to a roar. The problem was that with any of the other sketches, I could simply have done them badly. But if you do the "Silly Walks" badly, it's slightly funnier, so I had no control over the situation.

The other Pythons greeted me triumphantly as I left the stage, with smug know-it-all grins on their faces. And so I was stuck with it, all through the British tour, the Canadian tour, Drury Lane, City Center in New York, and finally the Hollywood Bowl. The only revenge available to me was that every night, on stage, as I stood up from my chair, and circled Palin, explaining how difficult it was to give him a grant to develop his Silly Walk, the audience were always laughing so loudly that they couldn't hear the dialogue. This enabled me to explain to Palin nightly, that the sketch we were doing was nothing like as funny as people thought, that it was, in fact, a rather weak piece of material, typical of the low-quality sketches normally written by Michael and Terry J, and that he was thoroughly lucky that Graham, Eric, and I had ever allowed him to be in the Monty Python team.

Indeed, throughout, Palin was the Python who caused me most trouble. One night, during the "Dead Parrot" sketch when he told me that although he did not have a replacement parrot, he was able to offer me a slug, I asked, as usual, "Does it talk?" He was supposed to say "…Not really." On the night in question he responded "…Well, it mutters a bit." Not particularly funny, but on this particular evening it hit a nerve, and I had to resort to the standard actors' trick of turning upstage to stare at the back cloth until I had got my giggles under control. This took a very long time. So long, that by the time I turned back to Michael to continue the sketch I found I had completely forgotten where we were…

So, I simply turned towards the stalls and asked them "What's the next line?" About sixty people shouted it out. At this moment I abandoned the script and embarked on a philosophical discourse, questioning the point of my behavior, standing in front of an audience performing a sketch the dialogue of which they knew better than I did. I then invited them all up on stage to do the sketch with Michael instead of me. But it was agreed that it would be too crowded. So I merely conducted them as they shouted out my lines, while Michael continued to perform his own.

Of course, comedy is all about the audiences. Right back at the start of the British tour, a few performances after the Brighton debacle, the show seemed to be in good shape. Then we did a matinee in Bristol, at the Hippodrome. Silence reigned. Nothing we did could interest the audience. As I sat in my dressing room listening over the Tannoy, I realized that the show was, of course, not funny. It was a strange feeling, discovering that none of the material worked. Fortunately, my state of shock only lasted about ninety minutes before the evening performance began. Now…hilarity! Screams of laughter greeted everything we did. The show was funny again, and we did not need a complete rewrite and midnight rehearsals of the replacement material. Phew!

But that's the way with comedy. You're down there in the sand and the blood. You can't talk about the interesting atmosphere, the fascinating ambiguities, or the meaning of the symbolism. It's either funny, or you're dead. That's why comedians "die" and actors don't.

MICHAEL PALIN: What I Remember

It was the early summer of 1973. We wore long hair and flares. (Except for John, who has never allowed his wardrobe to be dictated by the whim of fashion. I swear he's worn the same pair of trousers ever since I've known him.) In less than four years we had churned out forty television shows, three albums, two books, and a full-length feature film, *And Now for Something Completely Different*. We were hot. In fact we were *very* hot because three of us—Neil Innes, Terry Jones and myself—were in the back of a car with no air-conditioning, driven by a chauffeur with no sense of direction, driving aimlessly around the sterile approach roads to Birmingham in a queen mother of a Daimler. The driver was Sid. He was small, elderly, and myopic, and he was a Python character long before Python.

A few nights earlier the tour, which we had whackily and irreverently, called the *First Farewell Tour*, had opened, fairly disastrously, at the Gaumont Theatre, Southampton. All the sound cues, music, on-screen film inserts, and our radio mikes were the sole responsibility of just one engineer, Dave. He was, quite predictably, falling apart. He had not slept for a week and was kept going only by fear. The results were alarming and unpredictable. Film would come up without sound, music cues would spring out loud and clear in the middle of sketches, only to be hastily strangled. Worst of all, despite several days of rehearsal, Dave was still having serious trouble remembering our names. He would see two characters on stage and raise up the mikes hopefully on what, to his over-amphetamined brain, appeared to be a two-hander between Eric and Graham, only to find out it was Eric and me on stage, while the late, great Dr. Chapman, mike raised to the full by Dave, sat on the lavatory backstage, complaining to the entire auditorium about the fucking awful audience.

Anyway, the pressure of the tour was increasing Sid's inability to find the centre of Birmingham, or indeed anywhere. A few days later we found ourselves in Edinburgh. The distance from the theatre to the Post House Hotel was about two miles. Ten minutes' drive at the most, along the broad main Glasgow Road. After two hectic shows in one afternoon we flung ourselves into the back of the Daimler and Sid set out for our hotel. After twenty-five minutes we looked out on a bleak and desolated expanse of moorland, with the lights of Edinburgh far behind us. A sign flashed by in the gloom. "Peebles" it read.

"Is this the Glasgow Road, Sid?" one of us asked.

"I think so," said Sid.

"It said Peebles."

"Where did it say Peebles?" asked Sid with interest.

"On that road sign, Sid. On the sign on the side of the road."

Sid took this information with only mild interest.

"Turning just coming up," he said authoritatively.

Moments later we found ourselves in a narrow, dimly lit track between the grey pebble-dash houses of a new housing estate. Sid, ever-hopeful that this might be the link road between Scotland's two great cities, drove until he came to a brick wall. Only then did Sid accept that this was not the Glasgow Road. It was a cul-de-sac.

After the shows at the King's Theatre Glasgow, it was no better. A two-minute drive to the Albany Hotel, a journey almost impossible to cock up, took Sid nearly half-an-hour.

"I was confused by all the lights," he complained bitterly. As Glasgow on a Sunday night was not exactly Piccadilly Circus, we could only conclude that the lights he was referring to must have been traffic lights. Sid was now so consistently wrong that, as Neil Innes observed, "He makes a mockery of the law of averages." A sort of compulsive fascination kept us loyal to Sid's Daimler, until one morning we left the Leeds-Bradford Post House to travel back to London. At the start of the drive we came to a fast, straight main road. Two large signs faced us. One said "North" and the other "South."

Sid turned north.

For the final leg of the tour, Terry Jones and I chose to travel in the other car. This was driven by a man named Bill. Bill was of a similar age to Sid, but was a bigger, much more confident man. However, Bill insisted that we travel in convoy, with Sid, John, and Eric in front (Graham had his own personal chauffeur, a handsome young man, constantly pulling into lay-bys, where the occupants of the car could enjoy stiff gin and tonics). The idea of Bill following Sid seemed a prime example of an out of the frying pan into the fire situation, but Bill shouted over his shoulder that there was a reason for it. Sid's car wasn't working very well. The brakes were in a very dangerous state. It would have been nice to have been able to catch Sid up and warn his occupants of this, but Sid was touching 100 mph by then and Bill couldn't get near him.

Heavy rain hit us a few miles outside Bristol. Visibility was atrocious. Our windows were steaming up alarmingly. Occasionally we would catch a glimpse of Sid's Daimler through the murk. It was swaying about like a raft in a storm. Terry, now thoroughly alarmed by the ratio of velocity to visibility, suggested Bill might like to clear the windscreen so he could see out.

"It's just the rain. Nothing we can do about it," Bill assured him.

"It's a mist. It's on the inside," Terry persisted.

"Can't do anything about that," said Billy, cheerfully.

"Couldn't you just use the de-mister?" Terry asked, as condensation slowly entombed us.

Bill looked quite impressed at this.

"Where's that then?"

Terry pointed to a knob on the dashboard marked "Demister." Bill touched it warily and sure enough, after a moment or two, the windscreen began to clear. Bill shook his head in awed disbelief.

The Kamikaze Brothers finally got us to Bristol, and there, much to our relief, stood the ten-story bulk of the Dragonara Hotel. For some reason, ahead of us, Sid had pulled up at the curve. He dismounted from the Daimler and was standing in the road looking to left and right.

"Everything all right, Sid?"

"I'm looking for someone to ask where the bloody hotel is."

With one voice we all cried and pointed.

"It's there, Sid. It's there! Look! Across the roundabout at the bottom of the hill. It says 'Dragonara' in enormous letters!"

With a reproachful look as if to say, "You just put that sign there didn't you?" Sid climbed back into the Daimler and we progressed down the hill towards the hotel. At the bottom of the hill, almost unbelievably, Sid turned left, away from the hotel, over a low hill, in the direction of the docks.

At this point, those of us lucky enough to be in Bills vehicle fell back into our soft leather seats, hollering and hollering with mirth, disbelief and the satisfaction of knowing that, for once, we would get the first choice of rooms. We were close enough to the Dragonara Hotel to see the lights of the foyer when Bill swung away to the left and followed Sid towards the docks.

People often ask if there is any subject that we wonderful, wild, whacky, irreverent comedy mould-breakers would never tackle. The only one I can think of is chauffeurs.

TERRY JONES: What I Remember

$*$

●

---

* A single full stop may not seem much to have remembered, but considering the huge quantities of drugs that we all used to imbibe in those days, this is really quite a considerable feat of memory. In fact if one were to formulate an equation with what there was to remember on one side and all the hundreds and

135

thousands of kilos of cannabis, marijuana, ganja, hemp, hash, bhang, kef, grass, cocaine, basuko, crack, heroin, junk, smack, methadone, downers, uppers, siders, barbiturates, morphine, opium, amphetamines, dexies, LSD, Ecstasy, STP, on the other…

Oh! Hang on! Michael has just emailed me to remind me that we didn't take any drugs. I'd totally forgotten. Well! Well! Well! I've just emailed Michael again and he is quite positive that we didn't do drugs at all. How odd. You'd think performers of a whacky, off-the-wall, zany, madcap TV show like ours would have been stoned or out of our heads most of the time. But no! Michael says we were always pretty straight and couldn't even get too drunk if we were to get through the evening's performance. And now Eric's just rung to say the same thing…in fact he says as far as drugs were concerned most of us didn't even know where the aspirin was half the time. Terry Gilliam has just stuck his head through the ceiling and said he agrees. Although that can't be right. Surely the inventor of such whacky, off-the-wall, zany, madcap cartoons would have been out of his skull from the moment he got up to the moment he crashed out on somebody else's floor? But Terry G. says he had to work too hard getting the animations together to be able to spend time smoking dope or shooting up. And now I've just had John on a live video link from Los Angeles, where he's currently playing the lead in *Peter Pan The Musical*, and he agrees with the others. He told me: "We were all too anally retentive to use substances to relax, Terry baby, far out, man, see what I mean?"

Which leaves me with the problem, if we whacky, off-the-wall, zany, madcap performers weren't on drugs the whole time, why is a full stop the only thing I can remember about the *Monty Python* live stage shows?

I mean I can remember perfectly well what happened yesterday. Yesterday I…er…well…um…yesterday…I think I went for a walk with the dog…or was that the day before? Do I have a dog? Maybe it's a cat. It's downstairs! I'll go and have a look… Yes it *is* a dog! You see! So I was right, I must have taken it for a walk yesterday because if it was a cat I wouldn't have, would I? So you can see that I'm perfectly rational and in full possession of my faculties.

My dog has just informed me that I didn't take it for a walk yesterday or the day before and that if I don't take it out now it's going to burst…all over the floor. So I'd better go.

Oh! I've just remembered something that happened when we were doing the Hollywood Bowl show. I can't remember all the details but the thing I remember is the end. It was a full stop like this.

ERIC IDLE:
What I Remember

The question everyone asks is *Did we get along?* A typical touchy-feely question. I suppose the answer is: up to a point and certainly well enough. Any bunch of young men on the road are bound to have disagreements and arguments and fights and yes we probably killed a few people and left a few hearts broken and teenagers pregnant but for god's sake *a bunch of comedians on the road?* What do you expect? Were we weird? Of course we were. Did we take drugs? Only when offered. Were we drunk? Invariably. Is the sight of John Cleese having dinner alone at a small table for one in an empty restaurant a few tables from the rest of us bizarre? Of course it is. Was Graham Chapman frequently drunk and obnoxious to women? Only if crawling around the floor putting your hands up the skirts of strange girls and barking loudly is obnoxious. Of course he was. But more importantly we were funny.

I suppose it might be possible to find a group of decently behaved, church-going, polite young men touring the world doing eccentric skits about pressed meat products, but I very much doubt they would be as funny as we were. And that's not to boast. The audience insisted we were funny. They were laughing long before we came on. We began performing Python live only after we were already popular on TV, so our earliest audiences were discovering themselves as much as us. They already knew all about us, but who were these other people who roared along with them, who gave recognition applause to sketches, who laughed before we spoke: who the hell were they?

"Shut up" Cleese would yell at the audience "we haven't said anything funny yet."

To no avail. Might as well try and stop Liverpool supporters singing. They were there to enjoy themselves no matter what we did. One night the curtain went up in Winnipeg and the entire front row was dressed as a caterpillar. You can't lose a show like that.

Off stage and on Graham loved trying to shock, both in his activities and by his evident pleasure in recounting the details of his various escapades. In New York he once confessed to Mike and me that he had slept with a lady. We thought it over and said it was okay providing he didn't make a habit of it. His *Liar's Autobiography* is of course entirely truthful and we can all testify to the stunning appearance of Graham wheeling in a large African American gentleman in

a wheelchair as his dinner date at a posh Torquay hotel and insisting on sharing with us such graphic intimate details they instantly earned his guest the soubriquet of The Boston Startler. Who could forget Graham being flung out of a small suburban hotel in Munich for appearing at breakfast (*Schinken mit Käse*) with three shining faced young men, or the embarrassment of the young blushing *Hausfrau* who suggested he would be more comfortable at the Deutscher Ei just a short mince away? In his flamboyantly outrageous, drunken, homosexual behavior Graham would have made a perfect British spy.

On a flight to Vancouver John announced that he had had enough, there would be no more Monty Python for him. Graham spent the flight persuading us to continue without him, which we eventually did for six more TV episodes (Series Four) before I too had had enough. The only real effect was that John didn't join us on the trip to California. In 1973 that was a serious mistake. He missed a really good time in LA. But of course for legal reasons I cannot possibly divulge what went on.

Maybe next time.

GRAHAM CHAPMAN:
What He Remembered

The tour was going well. A success everywhere. I had pulled in Southampton, Oxford, and even Cardiff, though it posed a bit of a challenge, but, full of gin and the feeling of superiority over mortals which commonly afflicts the adulated, I had reached my zenith in a naughty and, to this day, illegal act upon the floor of an empty dressing room. The fact that this romance blossomed from love at first sight right through to mopping up in the ten minutes available between Acts I and II of *Monty Python's First Farewell Tour*, merely seemed to add piquancy to the occasion.

However, Sunderland was a toughie – only two entries in the *Gay Guide*, "open summer, weekends only." No point in even trying, I thought, on a Wednesday night in March. And so for the first time I went with the others to eat after the show. But I never felt happy in a place unless I'd scored. This thought nagged as I drank my way through the meal, and watched the others being interested in eating, chatting with wives and non-wives. I had more to drink, and decided to cross Sunderland off the map. On my way past the reception desk I said, "Good grief, there's no one to go to bed with…where are all the young men around here? This is absolutely dreadful." I went to my room and fell drunkenly onto the bed, alone.

I woke up at five o'clock in the morning to find the night porter in bed with me, nude. He wasn't particularly my choice of person, but under the circumstances he was welcome. He had let himself in with a pass key and, faithful to the hotelier's code, put the customer satisfaction first. The satisfaction was mutual and I even found myself wanting to stay in Sunderland, because as things would have it, most of the junior staff apparently has a similar devotion to duty…

We left Sunderland far behind, and as our Range Rover sped us on our way to Edinburgh at a cool 120 mph on the hard shoulder with hazard lights flashing, I handed the bottle of Glenfiddich pure malt whisky to the curiously pallid hitchhiker, saying, "I can't understand why nobody else is using this lane," and marveled at the splendid unpredictability of life.

In Edinburgh I was very naughty indeed…
Two young…etc.

We stopped off at Windermere for a night on our way down south from Glasgow. A reporter did an interview with Mike, Eric, and myself in my room. We all went out to eat but I got bored with eating: I wanted Sex! Sex! Sex! We walked halfway round Lake Windermere. Lifeless: not a soul. I went back to my room in the hotel to go to bed. There was a knock on my door. It was the interviewer.

He said, "Sorry to disturb you, I seem to have left my microphone."
I said, "I bet you only did that so you could go to bed with me."
He said, "Oh all right."
Whammo! Zap! There was no holding me now.
Stark staring raving Mad.

TERRY GILLIAM: What I Remember

On 22 July 2008, at 20:07, Eric Idle wrote to Terry Gilliam:
> What about a nice sketch then for the book?
> Or what it was like to hang suspended above the stage waiting to be shot by John Cleese?
> How I went from a Cheerleader like Bush to having my hand up the skirts of co-eds.
> I hope you are well and still not yet dead
> Its a good rumour to have
> Never hurt Paul McCartney
> E

From: Terry Gilliam To: Eric Idle
Sent: July 22, 2008, 12:41 P.M.
> Mysterious E
> Tell me more about the book. I have been away…
> deep inside my current nightmare.
> Would pages from my sketchbooks
> have any relevance?
> Who are you?
> TG

On 23 July 2008, at 02:33, EI wrote:
> All pages from any sketchbooks most welcome
> The book is called Monty Python Live and is about
> the six times we performed live with the sketches
> and photos
> Reminiscences are good but art invaluable
> E

Gilliam to Idle
> Just confronted disaster!
> I can't find my sketchbooks of that period!
> My memory is fucked and I have counted on the
> books to nudge my synapses. I'm still searching
> but, I may have to kill myself. Stay tuned.
> TG

Idle to Gilliam
> No need.
> They think you are dead anyway…
> Love
> E

Gilliam to Idle
> Dear editor

God knows how much I would love to be able to recount rollicking tales of life on the road with Python as we toured England and Canada – exposing sordid details of the group's backstage shenanigans, revealing how the long days and nights away from home led certain of the weaker individuals down

that dark and dangerous path that ends in involvement with the seedier, unclean species of farm animal. But, unfortunately, I was not there.

The Terry Gilliam the audience saw and the person seen in the film of the Hollywood Bowl show is not me! That man was a double I hired to impersonate me. His name was Derek. He wasn't very funny.

Now, it goes without saying that the others in the group were keen for me to be part of the spectacle and pressed me hard to join in, but my shame was too great to say yes.

On television or film, clever camera angles can disguise personal shortcomings, but the stage is brutal and unforgiving. There is nowhere to hide, no way to camouflage the fact that I was only 3'3" tall. That's right, ladies and gentlemen, three feet three inches…a gnat's rectal diameter short of a metre. A runt.

I'm older now and have learned to accept the cruel hand fate dealt me but, at that time, I was not emotionally ready for the world to know the truth.

I hope I haven't ruined the book.

Perhaps Oprah would like me to share my story with her vast and understanding audience…like Tom did.

I can still draw big.

143

NEIL INNES: What I Remember

Unlike touring with the Bonzos, which was done in a large American station wagon, *On the Road* with Python meant limousines! Eric and I shared a Daimler that would have been equally at home at a wedding or a funeral. Indeed, our driver, Sid, would have been more at home at a wedding or funeral. We were trying to get to the Post House Hotel, located outside Leeds, in rolling countryside. After a while it became clear to Eric and me that we were lost.

"I think we must have passed it," suggested Eric.

"You'd think they'd put up a sign," grumbled Sid as he reluctantly turned the big car around ten minutes later.

"Was that it?" I ventured, as a large building hidden by trees flashed by. It took another ten minutes to persuade him to reverse direction. Eric and I were now fully concentrating on our whereabouts. It was beginning to get dark and we had a show to do…

"There it is!" we cried out together as we swept past a driveway with a large sign saying "The Post House Hotel."

"Where?" demanded Sid, clearly in a world of his own.

"Back there!" we wailed. It took another fifteen minutes to persuade him to turn around and then another ten to find a suitable place. Realizing that we were no longer in control of our destinies, we got the giggles. And we were almost hysterical as he overshot the hotel entrance again.

"You'd think they'd put up a sign," he said as we finally swept majestically past the extremely large sign into the hotel grounds.

"Yes, you'd think they'd put up a sign," we agreed, wondering if there might a future for us in the Diplomatic Corps.

For the rest of the tour there was a competition to avoid Sid's car…

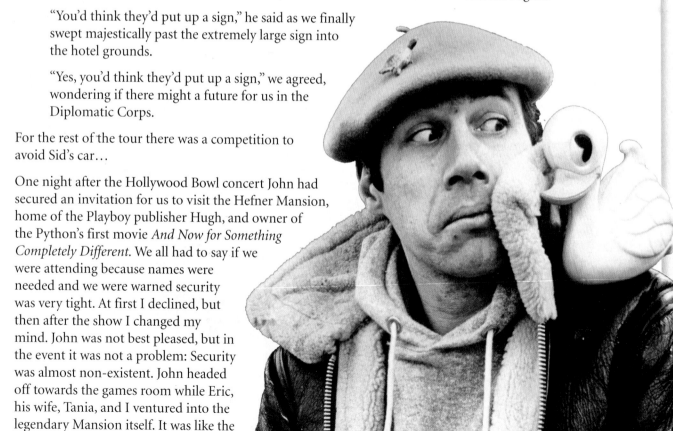

One night after the Hollywood Bowl concert John had secured an invitation for us to visit the Hefner Mansion, home of the Playboy publisher Hugh, and owner of the Python's first movie *And Now for Something Completely Different*. We all had to say if we were attending because names were needed and we were warned security was very tight. At first I declined, but then after the show I changed my mind. John was not best pleased, but in the event it was not a problem: Security was almost non-existent. John headed off towards the games room while Eric, his wife, Tania, and I ventured into the legendary Mansion itself. It was like the

Marie Celeste. Utterly deserted. Not a soul in sight. We found our way into a large bar, but there was no one there either. Intrepidly exploring the empty oak-paneled rooms, we finally found some waspish waiters gathered in a large kitchen.

"What are you doing *here*?" they demanded gaily.
"We're looking for a drink."
"Well, you need the bar."
"But there's no one there."
"Oh yes there is…"
"No there isn't."
"Go and look."

With the distinct feeling that this was not "a proper argument," we went and looked. And sure enough, as though nothing had happened, there was one of them, polishing a glass with an innocent look on his face.

"Now, what can I get you?"

A small shot of reality would have done me.

I left Tania and Eric at the bar and was taken on a guided tour by a very attractive "Playmate" with a skimpy dress and a comedy limp. This was fast becoming one of the most bizarre evenings of my life, and I've had a few. She showed me through the grounds and gardens to a large orangey grotto with plants and vines which held a vast indoor swimming pool sprinkled with discreetly lit split-level Jacuzzis.

"Who uses this place?"
"The guests."
"And who are the guests?"
"You are" she said nicely.

I was too weirded out to strip off and jump in. I've never felt more paranoid – and I've tried. And then suddenly I was on my own. My hobbling guide had vanished. Thinking the limo might still be waiting by the front door, I made my way through the shrubberies just in time to see Terry Gilliam drive up in his modest yellow "rental" car. I couldn't resist. I hid in the shadow of a tall conifer as he pulled up and parked a few feet from me. He got out, looking around the way movie directors do, and then I pounced…

"Aaarrrgggh!" I growled.

I'm not sure how many dancing teeth Conrad Poohs had, but that night Terry had many more and I saw every one of them.

"JEEEZZUSSS!" he finally exclaimed.

Life's like that – sometimes.

CAROL CLEVELAND:
What I Remember

Some of the happiest times I spent with the Pythons were when we were "on the road" together. I didn't do a great deal of socializing with them on the *Flying Circus* as they were far too smelly to be around at the end of a hot day of taping, but being thrown together away from home and away from the BBC gave me the chance to get to know them better. Plus of course, we could be as silly and outrageous as we wanted to be. I loved every minute of it!

Starting with *Monty Python's First Farewell Tour,* rushing from one place to the next, well it's all a bit of a blur to be honest. I don't remember all the theatres we performed in but I do remember all the restaurants we ate in. For me it was one, long gastronomical feast. All the fellas enjoyed fine dining, so while traveling in our limo from one venue to the next, we'd peruse Egon Ronay's Best Restaurant Guide and then seek them out. Having lived with an Italian for years, my knowledge of red wines didn't go much further than fruity Chianti, so I'll never forget that first £40 bottle of Burgundy I shared with them somewhere on the Yorkshire Moors. Thanks for the introduction, guys.

Later on we toured Canada (more food…huge steaks…my showgirl costume had to be let out twice). We started off in Toronto, where we played to an audience that didn't seem prepared for us, and when we introduced a new sketch, involving Terry Gilliam vomiting into a cocktail glass which was subsequently drunk by Michael, the curtain came down to an audible groan. I then had to come out front of stage and apologize for their behavior ending with "Honestly they're really so f****** sorry!" That went over like a turd in a punchbowl. At least the chaps had a good giggle backstage.

We really began to let our hair down on this tour and there were lots of laughs along the way…although not always with John, alas. He'd already announced his decision not to join the others in making another TV series and could, at times, be very grumpy and unsociable. He did however have his silly moments…as did we all. Like the evening we decided to behave like pop stars. (Well, why not? We were being treated as such.) We left the bar and headed for Mike's bedroom, where we jumped up and down on the bed, had a mad pillow fight, pushed furniture around the room, switched paintings and curtains from one place to another, rolled up the carpet, grabbed the TV and opened the window with a view to throwing it out…and then…we collapsed in a heap of laughter. So much for our attempt to trash the room…all *we* did was rearrange the furniture.

On another occasion a group of us returned late to our hotel and fancied a dip in the pool. We stripped down to our undies and jumped in, all except for Graham, who just stripped off! After our swim I handed out some towels but Graham said, "No thanks,"

and dashed out. He streaked, naked and dripping wet along the corridor towards the hotel lobby before disappearing up the stairs. At that moment an elderly couple appeared in the doorway and froze with open mouths. They must have thought they'd accidentally stepped into one of those infamous bath houses!

In 1976 we went to New York (the home of gargantuan sandwiches, and mouths to accommodate – showgirl costume let out once again!), where we played City Center. The audiences were getting bigger and bigger and again we got the full pop star treatment. I remember the first night, when we went to leave by the stage door and were greeted by a hundred screaming fans. One female rushed forward and swooned into Michael's arms. His face was a picture. (Poor little poppet.)

And then there was that scary, live, phone in radio show…All was going well until Graham started expounding the virtues of homosexuality. Not all New York gays were out of the cupboards yet and the whole tone of the show suddenly took a rather sinister turn. The presenter suggested we take just one last call when a Godfather voice came on the line with "You better watch your step…we don't like fags here… the Family's gonna get cha." The fellas thought it highly amusing but it sure put the frights up me.

For me the best was yet to come! Playing to our biggest audiences ever at the Hollywood Bowl in Los Angeles was an awesome experience, not least because I was going home. This was where I was brought up. The audiences were wild, crazy, and uncontrollable. Going out on stage and hearing eight thousand people speak your lines before you've even opened your mouth was, well…somewhat disconcerting at first. We decided to play with them, and on the second evening, instead of saying, "Would you like to come upstairs?" in the "Travel Agent" sketch, I said, "Would you like a blow job?" That fooled 'em. I have to say, the show did fall apart a bit here at times and there was quite a bit of giggling going on…not that the fans minded!

This would be the last time I'd join the Pythons on the road but I have some great memories. I always felt like I was the only girl in a naughty schoolboy gang. They'd tease me and talk me into doing things for their own amusement sometimes but they were always very protective. I love them all dearly.

Carol Cleveland FAQ

Q: So then *did* you?

A: You surely don't expect me honestly to answer that, do you?

Q: Why not? The guys did.

A: Really?! Oh…well…in that case…yes.

Q: You did?

A: Oh yes.

Q: How many of them?

A: All of them. Some of them twice. Even Terry Gilliam, though as he's American I did make him pay.

Q: Were they any good?

A: No. None of them. But several of them *were* quite funny. Except Terry Gilliam, who cried a lot.

Q: How many of them were gay?

A: All of them. Certainly the English ones. All Englishmen are gay.

Terry Gilliam is American but he is also a tremendous Anglophile and so is gay at weekends.

Q: I thought Graham was the gay one.

A: Graham was the *gayest*. But he was also the butchest. In fact I would never have guessed that he was really gay except he wouldn't put down his knitting.

Q: Were they nice to you?

A: No. Even in bed they behaved appallingly.

Q: How so?

A: Well Cleese for example wouldn't get off the phone. Michael Palin continued writing his diary and paused only to ask me to turn over. Terry Jones auditioned people while we were at it, and Eric Idle played guitar and gave interviews until he claimed to have "finished."

Q: Who had the longest?

A: Hard to tell. They were hung like satirists.

Q: Did you find them attractive in any way?

A: None of them were exactly babe magnets. More like fridge magnets. For me it was a job and I had to work very hard to keep it.

Q: Do they still stay in touch with you?

A: I have a restraining order on three of them, and the other two are still married and I have the Polaroids so they daren't come near me.

Q: Do you miss them?

A: No.

As well as appearing in the Flying Circus *TV series and their movies, Carol Cleveland also toured with the Pythons on the road and knows more about their personal and intimate habits than perhaps any other female (except possibly Dolores in Toronto).*

Python on Broadway

The whacky adventures of seven men and a girl who take a British Airways
Three Week "Make-U-A-Star" Bargain Holiday in New York.

And the promoter who lives to regret it.

April 6th, 1976:
Aboard British Airways 747 Super Transatlantic Jet Service (Better Food and More Leg Room Section)

Apparently a revolution has broken out in the Economy Class. Passenger's co-operatives have been formed and hand-luggage has been redistributed. There was sporadic firing during pre-lunch cocktails, but the hostesses say that everything is now under control. Trouble first flared over the definition of "wide-bodied comfort," but spread to include bitter criticism of Channel Six on the In-Flight Entertainment Programme. The latest word is that rows J to R are relatively quiet, but there is still isolated resistance from T 9–14 and four out of six rear toilets are still occupied.

Unfortunately several of the passengers are on *very* cheap holidays, and the steward has warned us to expect some trouble, but it's still a far-cry from the heady days of FLI-EEZI – "The Airline That Can't Afford To Crash." They sadly have become victims of the harsh economic realities of our times. Inflation and the general decrease in transatlantic passenger traffic hit them badly, and they could no longer afford rental payments in the hostess's uniform. In March they were forced to sell off their assets. The pride of the FLI-EEZI fleet, a 1940 Dakota, with a 1930 de Havilland wing and bits of a Shackleton Flying Boat, fetched £8, and the engine—an early, but still quite tough rubber band—fetched nothing. The pilot was forced to go back to being a waiter, and the waiters went back to being pilots for British Airways. A sad loss, as their cut-price, no noise, 17-day transatlantic glide fare, was easily the best value if you didn't have to be anywhere particular in the U.S.

At the time of writing, there is talk of them merging with another ambitious little airline, who have a hut near London Airport, but no-one to fly it. But the talk in the air at the moment is all of Concorde. Will it be allowed to land in New York, or will it be diverted to London? At present the British Government are pinning all their hopes on the chance of once yearly proving-flights to Butte, Montana. But the main problem that has to be faced is how to provide service that will justify a £650 ticket, especially when the seats on Concorde are so close together that only amputees can travel in total comfort. British Airways are hoping that the Queen herself will travel on most flights, to look after crying children, distribute blankets, and make cups of tea. Past Prime Ministers of Britain will bring round a solid-gold duty-free trolley, and the demonstration safety procedures at the start of the flight will be performed by the Royal Shakespeare Company, with Sir John Gielgud as the Hostess and Lord Olivier as the lifejacket.

In-flight entertainment will be provided by the Massed Pipes and Drums of the Uganda Police who will play a selection of the Small Faces' hits at your very own seat. At the end of the flight each passenger will be made a Dame Of The British Empire and given a free black and white television. In this sort of way the airlines hope that Concorde will eventually woo people away from boats, camels and rickshaws.

April 6th:
Kennedy Airport, New York City

On the ride in from Kennedy Airport we peer eagerly out from the windows of our enormous limousine (some of which is already in Manhattan) for signs of the awful bankruptcy of New York. There is nothing more guaranteed to lift the hearts and minds of English and Italians alike these days, than the news of somebody else going bankrupt.

On the flight from England the pound has dropped half a dollar, and those who came by Concorde would have made vast profits already. Sterling was badly hit today by the latest figures of the World's Most Economically Successful and Wonderful Nations, which show that Britain has slipped to 43rd position, behind Nicaragua and Las Vegas.

So how glad we are to see the horrific plight of New York City. Thousands of unemployed policemen roam the streets directing traffic and helping old ladies across the road, and in a desperate effort to cut back, many of the big banks are sharing motel rooms with each other. But it was when we arrived at our rented brownstone on East 49th Street, that the true extent of the city's newly acquired poverty was most clearly evident. Gone are the two uniformed attendants who would normally rush to the door of the limousine and bathe the tired traveler's feet in Oil of Olay, lifting him onto the back of the cheerful half-blind sage who would carry him to his front door, high above the dog shit, reciting the latest Wall Street prices in a high sing-song voice, whilst Tony Bennett or Mel Tormé struggled with your bags. Now the newly arrived visitor, thrown from his limousine, must fend for himself against a score of muggers, Jehovah's Witnesses, and Presidential candidates. Once past these he is confronted by ex-CIA men who thrust cards into his hand advertising back rooms where he can have his pink buttocks rubbed for only 25 dollars. How low can New York sink?

April 7th:
Sadie's Blue Groin Massage Parlour, 55th Street

It turns out to be 25 dollars *per buttock,* and if you want "more" it's up to you. It seems a lot to pay when you can still get corporal punishment free in many parts of the world, but I flash my American Express Card and the lady smiles appreciatively, and rejects it out of hand. "Cash or nothing, honey," she breathes with just a hint of a Latvian accent. Is it Howard Hunt? I have only sterling on me, and the sight of a pound note produces enormous mirth. Sadie reaches for a battered card headed "Currency Exchange Rates, Blue Groin Massage Parlour and International Conference Center 1976." It turns out the pound is worth 17 cents. "Of course we cannot compete with the banks"…she protests silkily. "But I like your ass, I give you 17 cents and a hamburger."

This complicated and wholly unethical transaction is completed, and she agreed to look after my 156 hamburgers whilst I am shown into a small cubicle, bare save for a small picture of Dwight Eisenhower. "You will have to take that off," purrs my hostess, as she gently slips the photograph from around my waist. "Ee was my favourite President, you know," she murmurs, tongue in my ear… "'im and Clemenceau.…" Her name is Dolores and she has a face like the early Mariner Pictures of the moon. She has a bugging device which keeps slipping out of her bra, and she asks me repeatedly if I am Dr. Kissinger, despite the fact that it's obvious I'm not. She notices this eventually and offers me instead a Special Bicentennial Massage and Good Time, but as this involves livestock, I settle instead for the simple Economy Rub and no finger work. After half an hour's massage I can hardly walk, but Dolores smiles a real Mare Tranquillitatis smile and says only Rocky Marciano lasted the full hour. By the time I get dressed I find that the pound has slipped to 12 cents and a hamburger with no ketchup.

As I leave I notice Muhammad Ali defending his World Heavyweight title for the 16th time this year, on the corner of 53rd and 7th. His opponent, a pimply shop assistant from Trenton, is reputedly getting 2 million dollars. Walk back to 49th Street via gardens of the nearby United Nations Building. Sit on a seat beside the East River which has been thoughtfully donated to "the citizens of New York, from the nations of the Third World." No sooner had I sat down than the seat split in two, there was a loud whirring sound and I was flicked high into the air and into the East River. A Mr. Moynihan of the River Police fished me out, and shook his fist at the seat, muttering angrily that there were limits to American generosity.

April 8th:
Broadway

So this is Broadway! The lights, the dirt, the glamour, the small brown stains on the sidewalk at the corner of 47th. All the Greatest Stars in the world wanted one day to be on Broadway, and here we were at last, haggling over the bill in the Stage Delicatessen. The trouble began earlier when we had wanted to sign a photo of Robert Redford and have it displayed in the window. The manager said that Robert Redford has already signed one. Foolishly, in retrospect, we insisted that we *were* Robert Redford. The manager picked us up on this almost immediately. "Hey..how come seven guys and a girl be Robert Redford, huh? You tell me that huh?" Eric embarked on a short but pithy treatise on Kierkegaardian theories regarding the nature of perception and reality, and we were thrown out. However we had not gone two blocks when the manager rushed after us, shouting that we hadn't left a tip, so we were hauled in again.

Who should we see at the table by the window but Robert Redford himself, signing pictures with the Kingston Trio? He called us over and introduced us to a friend of his, a Mr. D.P. Throat, who immediately accosted us with photos of the last six American Presidents in bed with each other, and interesting evidence linking President Ford's entire cabinet with one of New York's most popular zoo exhibits. He talked in a strange gravelly voice and was wearing an ancient Javanese tribal mask to avoid recognition.

To be truthful, there aren't many theatres on Broadway. They all seem to be a little *off* Broadway, but of course not as *off* Broadway as an Off-Broadway theatre would be. Our theatre was no exception. *On* Broadway, where it should have been, was a shop selling rubber gifts and Bicentennial underwear and other things to alleviate mental distress. "Could you tell me where the City Center Theatre is please?" I asked with an undeniable thrill of pride as I spoke the name. "Yeah," said the rubber goods seller, taking out his chewing gum and sticking it temporarily on an unsold copy of Ron Ziegler's first novel, "toin left into 55th by Onan's Deli, walk down past Bud's pretzel stand, right the way to de Budget-Rent-A-Car office, and ask there." I thanked him and walked off in the direction of 55th, passing Pearl Bailey on the way, who was looking very Minskoff. Things were very different at the Budget-Rent-A-Car office. For a start they recognized me, always flattering to an artist's ego, and even more when he is in search of his very own Broadway theatre. "Aren't you Tony Perkins?" I toyed with the idea of being Tony Perkins and decided: what the hell, if it'll please her that much, I'll be Tony Perkins. "How did you guess?" I returned playfully, with the sort of cute, apologetic half-smile Tony adopted so well in *The Trial*. "Well, you don't look like Woody Allen", she replied, and laughed. I laughed too. We both laughed. Then in came one of the boys who cleans the cars in the back garage, and he started to laugh too. Then the branch manager, Mr. Ron Shafelson, could be heard laughing in his office, and the lady at the other end of the reception desk began laughing and across the road there were peals of laughter from Bud's pretzel stand, and it was all going so well when… in walked Tony Perkins. I prayed no-one would recognize him. Fortunately no-one did, and after pouring himself a drink from the iced water machine (rather self-consciously, I thought), he swept out with a sort of "huh!"

"Well, who was *he*?" grimaced the lady at the other end of the reception desk sourly.

"Well he certainly wasn't Woody Allen," I replied, and she collapsed in a wild, honking, dress-splitting holocaust of mirth, flinging her laughter wracked body this way and that until the counter was covered in a thick spume-flecked veneer. But the laughter turned to sobbing, the sobbing to remorse and recrimination – she hadn't wanted to work for Budget-Rent-A-Cars, not at this branch anyway. She'd been repeatedly passed over for parts in Marty Scorsese movies, and her husband Wilf had made a complete fool of himself by standing as a favorite son candidate in the Iowa Primary. Mr. Shafelson was so moved by her story that he closed the office half an hour early, and told me rather curtly that, just because I was Tony Perkins, it didn't give me the right to walk into any car rental office and mess up one of the staff emotionally.

I decided to stop looking for the theatre that day and put an ad in the paper, asking for anyone with any knowledge of City Center to let me know. Walking slowly home up 7th Avenue I noticed that New York is alive with good ideas this Bicentennial Year: on the corner of 54th there's a place where you can have a Bicentennial Look Into A Darkened Room for only 12 dollars, and right next door, I stop and buy what are purported to be the underpants worn by Herbert Hoover when setting up the Tennessee Valley Authority. They are No. 19 in a series of Great Underpants of History. Others include the ones Chamberlain was wearing when he returned from Munich in 1938, the pair that Ed Muskie campaigned in for much of 1972, and an enormously droopy pair worn by Marshal Bulganin and others.

April 9th:
The Russian Tea Room

There's always a fair sprinkling of the famous and fortunate in here, so we're told: one of the Kennedys or an Old Testament prophet at the very least, but tonight it's quiet. A pall of ordinariness hangs, like a major "Scoop" Jackson policy speech, over the Russian Tea Room tonight. It's all very well for the waiters to tell us that Diana Ross is crouching over behind the coat-racks, or that John Wayne's in the men's room when all we can see are the tables full of Bank Americards. How different it all is from the original Russian Tea Room in Smolensk. There, on a good night, say after a Revolution, even Lenin might have to queue for a table. Leon Trotsky would be gesticulating fiercely over an untouched plateful of blinis. Dzerzhinsky, Stalin and Rykov, the new Commissioner for the Interior, would have reached the coffee stage, and over by the window Martov and a tableful of Mensheviks would be hunched defensively over cherry pancakes, drinking rather too much Caspian Burgundy and bitterly wondering what happened to the Marxian two-stage theory of capitalist development. Then a buzz of excitement, as the burly but unmistakable figure of Grigori Zinoviev, newly appointed President of the Leningrad Soviet, strides in, leaving a greatcoat so heavy that the hat-check girl (soon to be Stalin's wife) can hardly lift it. Kamanev shouts a raucous Marxist Leninist greeting at his newly-arrived colleague.

"We did it! We led a successful proletarian revolution!"

"Now we must consolidate!" yells Trotsky, spitting a hail of blinis over his friend.

April 12th:

Two days to opening night and we still can't find the theatre. If we don't find it by 7:30 on Wednesday, it could be disastrous for the show. Think of the reviews. "The curtain didn't rise once throughout the evening, no-one turned the lights on, and the audience had to break in through the men's room window," Clive Barnes. "Absolutely no-one there" N.Y. *Daily Post*. "We sat there for six hours before being cleared out by police. If this is British Comedy thank God we won the War of Independence," *Le Monde*. "Didn't see a thing for two hours, but I *was* in the cheap seats," *Esquire* magazine. Perhaps the theatre doesn't exist. Or perhaps it has been sold by the city of New York to pay their debts. Our theatre could at this moment be on board ship en route to create an Arab Broadway in Jeddah or Bahrain. The trouble is Arab Broadway is a contradiction in terms, and would almost certainly result in another Middle East War – directed by Gower Champion.

It's getting very hot too. 96 degrees. The *New York Times* claims it's the hottest-ever April day in New York. On Park Avenue business men in light cotton suits keep bursting into flame, and in Sam Goody's on 5th Avenue, the Country and Folk albums have melted into the Light Classical section, giving weird misshapen 29½-inch LP's of Dolly Parton singing Tchaikovsky.

April 13th:
Breakfast on 2nd Avenue

"Whatdya want?"

"Er…" but he's gone. What a fool I am. No-one in New York ever says "Er…" except President Ford, and he's not here very often. Decide to read the Sunday Paper to see if there's any mention of the theatre. Taking a couple of deep breaths and supporting my right leg against the steel table leg, I manage to hoist the paper onto the table at the second attempt.

"O.K. Whattdya want?"

"Well…"

"Ah, for Chrissake, hurry *up*."

"I'llhaveorangejuicetwoeggsbaconpotatoesandcoffeeplease!"

"O.K." He whips the menu away and over to the lady on the next table who's been waiting around for at least four-fifths of a second. As he does so he dislodges a 947-page Bloomingdales Spring Bargains section from the paper, which falls off the table onto my right foot, slightly chipping the bone.

"Aarrghh!"

"Yeah, whaddizzit?"

"Nothing…nothing, just a cry of pain. Sorry"

"You wanna hospital not a restaurant!" he sympathizes sharply as he slaps a plate of bagels in front of me.

"Excuse me…"

"Whadizzit? D'you wanna dance?"

"No…it's just that I didn't order…"

"You want *mushrooms* with the bagels?"

"No…it's just that I wanted…"

Forty-eight seconds and five helpings of bagels-with-mushrooms later, I'm out on 2nd Avenue and heading for Broadway. Halfway there, I remember I haven't left a tip, and my wife and children are alone in the house. The cab driver says that for an extra tip, he'll take the tip over for me. What a decent chap.

April 14th:

Only four hours to go to opening night, and at last a lucky break. We bump into Yasser Arafat signing photos of Robert Redford in the Stage Delicatessen. He remembers having seen a City Center Theatre somewhere on 55th.

We hurry off up Broadway, passing Muhammad Ali defending his title yet again, this time in a subway

154

entrance on the corner of 51st. Ali's reputed to be getting 904 million dollars for this fight, and the two old ladies he's fighting will share 20 million.

Opening Night!

Now at last I know some of the excitement that Katharine Hepburn and Ethel Barrymore and Barbra Streisand must have felt. The constant changing of underwear, the sound of a thousand flushing toilets, as the minutes tick by bringing ever nearer the moment when you step out on the Broadway stage for the first time! In my dressing room, I struggle into my costume, banging my head on the half-loose hook that Nureyev probably banged his head on, scrubbing the scum out of the washbasin the way Joan Fontaine and Elizabeth Taylor must once have scrubbed. Was that cigarette butt in the water glass once smoked by Henry Fonda and did Jeanne Eagels herself stuff that tissue paper in the ventilating system?

Of course some things have changed. Instead of the head round the dressing-room door, and the cheery shout "Ten minutes, Mr. Palin!" there is a booming distorted barrage of sound over the intercom which could be the mating cry of the orange-rumped agouti, or the arrival of a flight from Karachi. It's the five minute call.

Excitement and tension grip backstage like a vise. Underwear is changed for the last time. Our promoter sells his last Biro out on the sidewalk, and shuffles in to wish us luck. For him and all of us, this is it…

Unfortunately, we open on Passover night, thus losing the Jewish element of the audience. The Stalls are entirely empty, but halfway through the third number we hear someone moving about at the back of the second Circle. A search by theatre staff reveals a small party of Canadians and word has it that there is a Pole up in the Balcony. But the show goes well. No typhoons hit the theatre, and there are no scalpings.

May 5th, 1976

Despite our poor record of hygiene, they let us stay on at the City Center for three more weeks. The time passes pleasantly enough, except that we are constantly pestered by representatives of *Esquire* magazine – over the phone, at parties, and sometimes even in broad daylight. Occasionally they adopt disguises and talk in "funny voices" in order to trick us into writing for them. I spent one enormously enjoyable evening with Yehudi Menuhin and his "wife," talking over art, culture, music, theatre and life generally, only to find out later that they were both assistant editors of *Esquire* magazine wearing Yehudi Menuhin and his "wife" masks.

But it was on the plane back to England that they made their final attempt to get "copy," when an *Esquire* Editor-in-Chief, wearing a *Cosmopolitan* assistant editor's mask, forced his way into the galley and threatened to blow himself and all the salads to pieces unless he received an article entitled "Python on Broadway." So, the salads were saved, but sadly not the readers of Esquire…

Michael Palin July 8th, 1976
for *Esquire* magazine

Great Moments in British Acting

How to Be a Great Fucking Actor

By JAMES LIPTON TEABAG

Volume III
"Noses"

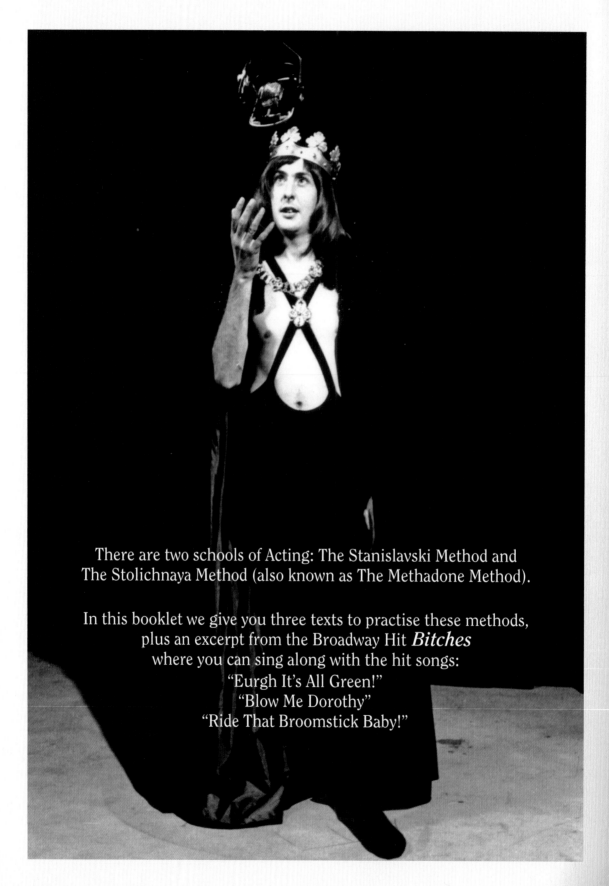

There are two schools of Acting: The Stanislavski Method and
The Stolichnaya Method (also known as The Methadone Method).

In this booklet we give you three texts to practise these methods,
plus an excerpt from the Broadway Hit **Bitches**
where you can sing along with the hit songs:
"Eurgh It's All Green!"
"Blow Me Dorothy"
"Ride That Broomstick Baby!"

How to Be a Great Fucking Actor*

Originally published as How to Be a Great Drama Queen

By JAMES LIPTON TEABAG

Welcome Executive Actors!

This is the Complete Monty Python Acting Kit.

And it includes:

- ◆ Excerpts from **Drama Queen for Beginners**
- ◆ Action-packed scripts for you to rehearse in your own bathroom mirror
- ◆ Costume Hints on How To Stuff Your Undies
- ◆ A guide to talking bullshit for TV interviews
- ◆ An Award Acceptance Speech
- ◆ A How to Be a Great Fucking Actor Dressing Gown

• •

Yes! Now you can bring the glitter and glamour of Broadway, The West End
and Hollywood Boulevard to your own front lounge.

Follow these simple instructions and impress your friends at
Parties, Masonics and Bar Mitzvahs

Or try it with your wife, or boyfriend (or both together)
and see them watch entranced
as **YOU** become
Sir Anthony Hopkins and Sir Ian McKellen and Tom Cruise all rolled into one.

159

All right, let's start with something very simple for actors.
In this play you will play the part of the drunk.
You'll need a bottle of vodka and some mixers.

Play 1: A Taste of Evil
by a very good bearded playwright

Montague de Vere .... *A zany Marxist Tycoon*
Sergeant Spencer & Superintendent Donaldson .... *Police Officers*
Cyril Prepuce .... *A Gardener and a Humanist*
George .... *Anthea's brother*
Anthea .... *George's sister*
Wong-Fu-Sun .... *A German Sinophile*
Tiger Woods .... *A Golfer*
Lady Veronica Caldwell .... *A lapsed Hindu Lap Dancer*
Brian "Monkeyglands" Johnson .... *A TV Quizmaster*
Dolores E. Mozart .... *A Winch Operator*
"Tiny Mike" O'McGear
Abdul Karim
Mrs. Thatcher .... *Not in This Play*
Miss World 1998
Madonna
Paul and Barry Spinoza .... *Also Not in This Play*
You .... *You*

SCENE ONE

A Police Station near Wolverhampton

SERGEANT SPENCER is at his desk; SUPERINTENDENT DONALDSON enters left.

SPENCER:	Morning, Super.
DONALDSON:	Morning, wonderful.
SPENCER:	Nasty business up at the Towers, sir.
DONALDSON:	Oh yes, what's happened?
SPENCER:	Montague's shot himself.
DONALDSON:	Dead?
SPENCER:	'Fraid so sir, blood everywhere…
DONALDSON:	All right Spencer, get onto the Yard while I get 'round to the Towers…*(he turns to go)*
YOU:	Hic.
DONALDSON:	Did you say something?
SPENCER:	No.
DONALDSON:	Must be the wind.
SPENCER:	Would you like to borrow my Tums?
YOU:	Hic.
SPENCER:	Or are you going past a sweetshop on the way, sir?
DONALDSON:	Yes, I'm going the pretty way, up through Tinkerbelle Wood.
SPENCER:	Get us some jelly babies then, sir.
DONALDSON:	Okay.
YOU:	Hic.

He exits.

SCENE TWO

The Morning Room at The Towers.

MONTAGUE lies in a pool of blood behind a heavy curtain which completely conceals his body.
ANTHEA and GEORGE are pacing the room.

ANTHEA:	Don't torture yourself, George.
GEORGE:	(*slamming the door on his fingers*) I'm sorry, my dear.
ANTHEA:	Ever since we arrived at The Towers, I've had this terrible feeling…
GEORGE:	(*putting his head in the piano and dropping the lid on it*)…Of what, my dear?
ANTHEA:	I don't know, it's as though…as though…

The door to the garden opens.

CYRIL enters holding a smoking gun, a blood-stained assegai, a tangled length of nylon stocking,
a gas oven, an empty bottle of poison, a book of famous murders, and an acid bath.

CYRIL:	Hello, everybody. I've just been re-laying the croquet lawn.
YOU:	Hic.

End scene…

Well now you've *got your feet wet,* as we say in the business, *it's time to move on to a more substantial part* (as the bishop said to the actress). In this play **YOU** have a much bigger part.

Play 2: All Quiet on the Western Front

Adapted by Frank Lampard and Jean Genet
From an idea by Hedy Lamarr

Charles De Vere Flyffe .... *A young Subaltern (You)*

Belinda Fforbes-Ttrenchh.. *A young Public-School Girl*

Ratso Rizzo .... *A character in* Midnight Cowboy

Mireille Biggs .... *A TV Quizmaster*

Harry "Four Eyes" Da Vinci Code .... *A CIA Agent*

Johnny Levin .... *A William Morris Agent*

"Sapper" McGough .... *A young Sapper*

Milos Gorman .... *On Wednesdays and Saturday matinees*

SCENE ONE
Enter **YOU** *as You.*

BELINDA:	Oh Charles! Charles! Charles!
YOU:	(*joyfully*) Belinda!
BELINDA:	Oh Charles!
YOU:	(*happily, yet with a hint of anxiety*) Belinda!
BELINDA:	I never thought I'd see you again.
YOU:	(*cryptically, with the merest trace of forced insouciance*) I'm on leave.
BELINDA:	Oh that's wonderful news…but why? Are you…?
YOU:	(*abruptly, almost defiantly, with an unaccustomed annoyance*) Yes.
BELINDA:	Where?
YOU:	(*deliberately and without bitterness*) In the toe.
BELINDA:	Oh no!
YOU:	(*enquiringly, yet with a hint of profound emotion detectable through the mask of innocence*) Belinda?
BELINDA:	Yes Charles?
YOU:	(*a strange diffidence mingling with tenderness*) I love you.
BELINDA:	I love you too.
YOU:	(*cautiously, affecting a delicately studied nonchalance*) But…
BELINDA:	But what? Can you still…?
YOU:	No. (*Tersely, yet softly, with a hint of weariness in a voice from which time has erased the hard edges of anger*) It's been shot off.
BELINDA:	Shot off?
YOU:	(*momentarily pausing only to achieve a deliberate flatness as if in silent reproach for her incredulity*) Shot off.
BELINDA:	Completely?
YOU:	(*helplessly, yet proudly, a telltale suggestion of remorse severing the thin thread of hope that has until this moment survived despite itself*) I'm afraid so.
BELINDA:	Oh Charles.
YOU:	(*beseechingly, longingly, with only a slight querulousness in the voice betraying a hint of the anxiety and self-doubt which he has inevitably suffered*) Oh Belinda!
BELINDA:	Charles!
YOU:	(*wistfully and imploringly, with overtones of melancholy and quizzical introspection clouding the once-eager freshness of his passionate emotions*) Belinda!
BELINDA:	Charles!
YOU:	(*half-crying, half-laughing, with a violent passivity, redolent of the self-mockery of a primeval anguish, expressing, in a word, all the extremes of human emotion, all the levels of attainment to which the mind can aspire in the eternal quest for the elusive goal of self-perfection*) Belinda!

CURTAIN: (a sheet or traveling rug will do).

163

That was very good. Now it's time for **Improv!**

This is the Actors' favorite as they don't have to remember any words and they need never stop talking.

In this Scenario, imagine you are a Tree and say whatever comes into your head.

Remember, *don't under act*!

And Cue!

You might want to try this in several other ways...
  A. As an orange
  B. As a wafer-thin mint
  C. As a Frenchman

PUBLICITY!

Perhaps the most important part of an Actor's Role is being interviewed on television.
Here is a simple example by a Great Actor on a British television show.

ALAN: Sir Edwin, which has been for you the most demanding of the great Shakespearean tragic heroes that you've played?

SIR EDWIN: Well this is always a difficult one, but I think the answer must be Hamlet.

ALAN: Which you played at Stratford in 1963?

SIR EDWIN: That's right, yes, I found the role a very taxing one. I mean, *Hamlet* has eight thousand two hundred and sixty-two words, you see.

ALAN: Really?

SIR EDWIN: Oh yes. Othello's a bugger too, mind you, especially the cleaning up afterwards, but he has nine hundred and forty-one words *less* than Hamlet. On the other hand, the homey's got more pauses, sixty-two quite long ones, as I recall. But then they're not so tricky, you see. You don't have to do so much during them.

ALAN: You don't?

SIR EDWIN: No. No, not really. And they give you time to think what sort of face you're going to pull during the next speech so that it fits the words you're saying as far as possible.

ALAN: How many words did you have to say as King Lear at the Aldwitch in '52?

SIR EDWIN: Well, I don't want you to get the impression it's just a question of the number of words. Getting them in the right order is just as important. Old Peter Hall used to say to me, "They're all there already— now we've got to get them in the right order." And, for example, you can also say one word louder than another, "To BE or not to be," or "To be OR not to be," or "To be or not to BE," you see? And so on.

ALAN: Inflection.

SIR EDWIN: And of course inflection. In fact, Lear has only seven thousand and fifty-four words, but the real difficulty with Lear is that you've got to play him all shaky legs and pratfalls and dentures falling out, 'cause he's ancient as hell, and then there's that heart-rending scene when he goes right off his nut—you know, "biddle dee dee diddle dee bibble dee dee dibble beep beep beep," and all that, which takes it out of you, what with having the crown to keep on. So Lear is tiring, although not difficult to act, because you've only got to do despair and a bit of anger, and they're the easiest.

ALAN: Are they? What are the hardest?

SIR EDWIN: Oh…fear.

ALAN: Fear?

SIR EDWIN: Mmm, yes, I've never been able to get that right. I can't do the mouth. I look all cross—it's a very fine line. Jealousy can be tricky…but for me, the most difficult is being in love—you know, that open-mouthed, vacant look that Vanessa Redgrave's got off to a tee. Can't do that at all. And also I'm frightfully awkward when I try that happy prancing, you know. Which is a shame, really, because otherwise Romeo's quite good for me—only three thousand and eight words and quite a lot of climbing and kissing.

ALAN: Sir Edwin—get stuffed.

All right NOW it's your turn…

165

Imagine you are on *Late Night with Jimmy Letterfergusonan**

*not a real name

LETTERFERGUSONAN: My next guest is an actor.
But none the worse for that.
(Audience laughs) Will you welcome please…
(Your name here.)

YOU: Hello. Great to be here.

LETTERFERGUSONAN: *He says something very funny off the cue card.*

YOU: *Laugh generously.*

LETTERFERGUSONAN: But seriously don't you ever get tired of acting?

YOU: Yes. I go to bed occasionally.

LETTERFERGUSONAN: *(smirks)* I know, I read the tabloids.

Audience laughs knowingly.

YOU: *Laugh generously.*

LETTERFERGUSONAN: *(mock outrage)* Stop it. It was his *Granny.*

Audience wet themselves.

YOU: *Smile politely. This too will pass…*

LETTERFERGUSONAN: Now you're currently appearing in…

YOU: In court!

LETTERFERGUSONAN: Ha ha ha. Apart from that…

YOU: In the CBS pilot *The Caves of Passion.*

LETTERFERGUSONAN: Let's hope it wasn't the same pilot who flew me back from Vegas. Seriously though. It's great to have you on the show. And all the best with it, son. We'll be right back with Cher.

The building site version of *Wuthering Heights*

166

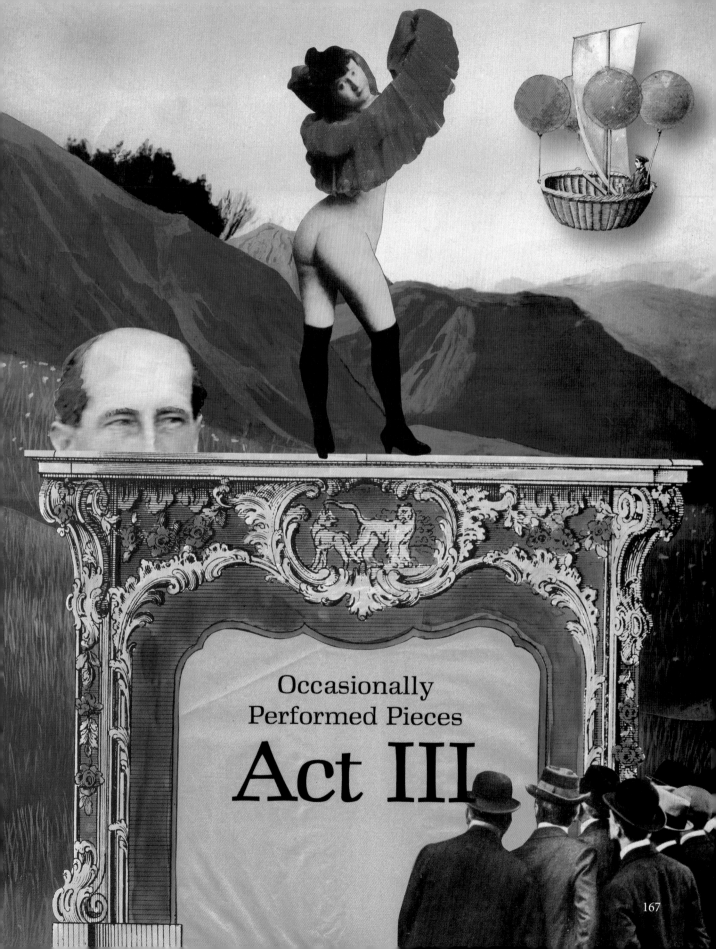

Occasionally
Performed Pieces
Act III

167

Anagrams

INTERVIEWER

Hello, good evening and welcome to another edition of *Blood, Devastation, Death, War and Horror*, and later on we'll be meeting a man who *does* gardening. But first on the show we've got a man who speaks entirely in anagrams.

NAM

Taht si crreoct.

INTERVIEWER

Do you enjoy it?

NAM

I stom certainly od. Revy chum so.

INTERVIEWER

And what's your name?

NAM

Hamrag. Hamrag Yatlerot.

INTERVIEWER

Well, Graham, nice to have you on the show – and where do you come from?

NAM

Bumcreland.

INTERVIEWER

Cumberland?

NAM

Staht sit sepricly.

INTERVIEWER

Now you've been doing this anagram version of Shakespeare…

NAM

Sey sye – taht si crreoct, ta the mnemot I'm wroking on *The Mating of the Wersh*.

INTERVIEWER

The Mating of the Wersh. By William Shakespeare?

NAM

Nay, by Malliwi Hakespearse.

INTERVIEWER

What else?

NAM

Two Netlemeg of Verona, Twelth Thing, The Chamrent of Venice…

INTERVIEWER

Have you done *Hamlet*?

NAM

Thamle? "Beot or bot neot, that is the nestoqui."

INTERVIEWER

And what are you working on at the moment?

NAM

Ring Kichard the Thrid.

INTERVIEWER

I'm sorry?

NAM

"A shroe, a shroe! My dingkome for a shroe!"

INTERVIEWER

Ah, Ring Kichard…er, but surely that's not an anagram that's a spoonerism.

NAM

If you're gonna split hairs I'm gonna piss off.

Bee Keeper

INTERVIEWER

Good evening. Tonight we're taking a look at bee-keeping and to tell us all about it we have in the studio a man who's been keeping bees for over forty years, Mr. Reggie Prawnbaum. Good evening, Mr. Prawnbaum.

BEE-KEEPER

Good evening.

INTERVIEWER

What first interested you in the bee world Mr. Prawnbaum?

BEE-KEEPER

Well even as a child I used to…

INTERVIEWER

Shhhhh.

BEE-KEEPER

I'm sorry, shouldn't I have said that?

INTERVIEWER

No of course you should. Pay no attention please, when I say shhhh it's just a nervous habit I picked up. If I want you to keep quiet I shall say shush.

BEE-KEEPER

Oh I see. Um, even when I was a child I used to wander around.

INTERVIEWER

Shh.

BEE-KEEPER

Oh I'm sorry…I used to wander round the fields watching the bees flying from flower to flower.

INTERVIEWER

Shh.

BEE-KEEPER

And taking note of the flowers they visited.

INTERVIEWER

Shush.

BEE-KEEPER

Was that wrong?

INTERVIEWER

I'm sorry, did I say shush? I mean shh. Do go on, it's very interesting.

BEE-KEEPER

And I have grown to love the little…

INTERVIEWER

Shh.

BEE-KEEPER

…creatures. Nature really has produced a little masterpiece
in the life of the bee.

INTERVIEWER

SQUAWK. I'm so sorry. I'm afraid that's a reflex action too.
I squawk every time someone mentions the word life. SQUAWK.
You see, even when I mention it. I should have told you. Please go on.

BEE-KEEPER

Oh very well. As we all know bees are divided into…

INTERVIEWER

Shh.

BEE-KEEPER

Different categories.

INTERVIEWER

Shh.

BEE-KEEPER

The queen for example, unlike the worker bee, whose life span…

INTERVIEWER

SQUAWK.

BEE-KEEPER

Living expectancy is only one year.

INTERVIEWER

Shh.

BEE-KEEPER

The worker bees on the other hand have a much longer.

INTERVIEWER

SHUSH.

BEE-KEEPER

Do you want me to stop?

INTERVIEWER

Yes, you were just about to say life SQUAWK.

BEE-KEEPER

No I wasn't.

INTERVIEWER

Oh I'm sorry, please continue.

BEE-KEEPER

The workers have a much longer life.

INTERVIEWER

SQUAWK.

BEE-KEEPER

I'm sorry, I wasn't meaning to say that, it's just that you've got me rattled.

INTERVIEWER

Shh.

BEE-KEEPER

Well the queen bee stays in the hive and the workers…

INTERVIEWER

Shh.

BEE-KEEPER

Fly around from flower…

INTERVIEWER

Shh.

BEE-KEEPER

To flower collecting the pollen.

Interviewer runs out.

BEE-KEEPER

…What's happened?

PRODUCER

Don't worry please, I'm the producer. I'm afraid the interviewer is going to explode. We should have warned you but he explained to us that he would explode if anyone said the word pollen.

BEE-KEEPER

Oh I see.

Explosion.

Children's Story

Storyteller is sitting with a large children's book.

MAN

Hallo, children, hallo. Here is this morning's story. Are you ready?
Then we'll begin.

Opens book. Reads.

"One day Ricky the Magic Pixie went to visit Daisy Bumble in her tumbledown cottage. He found her in the bedroom. Roughly he grabbed her heaving shoulders, pulling her down onto the bed and…hurriedly…"

Reads silently puzzled. Then turns over a page quickly, smiles nervously.

"Old Nick the Sea Captain was a rough tough jolly sort of fellow. He loved the life of the sea and he loved to hang out down by the pier where the men dressed as ladies…"?

He reads on silently. A stick enters and pokes him. He starts and turns over the page.

"Rumpletweezer ran the Dinky Tinky shop in the foot of the magic oak tree by the wobbly dum dum bush in the shade of the magic glade down in Dingly Dell. Here he sold contraceptives and various things…discipline?…naked…"?

Without looking up.

That's all for today, children.

Reads a bit.

"With a melon"!?

173

Butcher's Shop

A City Gent enters.

GENT

Good morning, I'm interested in purchasing a chicken.

BUTCHER

Don't come in here with that posh talk, you stuck-up twit.

GENT

I beg your pardon?

BUTCHER

A chicken, sir. Certainly.

GENT

And how much does that work out per pound, my good fellow?

BUTCHER

Per pound, you slimy trollop, what kind of a ponce are you?

GENT

I'm sorry?

BUTCHER

Four and six a pound, sir, nice and ready for roasting.

GENT

Oh and I'd care to purchase some stuffing in addition, please.

BUTCHER

Use your own, you great poovey ponager.

GENT

What?

BUTCHER

Here you are, sir, and the stuffing.

GENT

Oh, thank you.

BUTCHER

"Oh thank you" says the great queen like a la-di-dah poofta.

GENT

I beg your pardon?

BUTCHER

You're very welcome, sir, call again.

GENT

Excuse me.

BUTCHER

What is it now, you great pillock?

GENT

Well I couldn't help noticing that you insult me and that you're polite alternately.

BUTCHER

I'm terribly sorry to hear that, sir.

GENT

Oh, that's all right.

BUTCHER

Just as well it is, you nasty spotted prancer.

Hungarian Phrase Book

A Hungarian Gentleman enters a tobacconist's. He is reading from a phrase book.

HUNGARIAN GENTLEMAN

I will not buy this record. It is scratched.

TOBACCONIST

I'm sorry?

HUNGARIAN GENTLEMAN

I will not buy this record. It is scratched.

TOBACCONIST

No…this…Tobacconist's.

HUNGARIAN GENTLEMAN

Ah! I will not buy this Tobacconist's. It is scratched.

TOBACCONIST

No. No…Tobacco…er…Cigarettes?

HUNGARIAN GENTLEMAN

Cigarettes. Yes, yes. *(Looking in book)*
Ah! My hovercraft is full of eels.

TOBACCONIST

What?

HUNGARIAN GENTLEMAN

(miming matches)

My hovercraft is full of eels.

TOBACCONIST

(showing some)

Matches?

HUNGARIAN GENTLEMAN

Yah, yah. *(He takes cigarettes and matches and pulls out loose change)*
(He consults book) Er…do you want to come back to my place bouncy bouncy?

TOBACCONIST

I don't think you're using that right.

HUNGARIAN GENTLEMAN

You great poof.

TOBACCONIST

Six and six…

HUNGARIAN GENTLEMAN

If I told you you had a beautiful body would you hold it against me?
I am no longer infected.

TOBACCONIST

(miming that he wants to see the book)

May I? *(He takes book)* It costs six shillings…*(Mumbling as he searches)*
Costs…six shillings. Ah! Uandelvayasha gridenwi strovenka.

H.G. hits the tobacconist. Policeman enters.

POLICEMAN

What's going on here then?

HUNGARIAN GENTLEMAN

(opening book and pointing at Tobacconist)

You have beautiful thighs.

POLICEMAN

What?

TOBACCONIST

He hit me.

HUNGARIAN GENTLEMAN

Drop your panties, Sir Arthur, I cannot wait till lunchtime.

POLICEMAN

Right! *(Grabs him and drags him out)*

HUNGARIAN GENTLEMAN

(as he goes)

My nipples explode with delight.

– Blackout –

The Dirty Fork

A smart restaurant.

MAN

Sorry I'm late, dear.

LADY

That's all right. I'm twenty minutes late myself.

MAN

Well let's not start worrying yet.

LADY

It's nice here, isn't it?

MAN

Yes, it's a very good restaurant. Five stars you know…

LADY

Really?

MAN

Oh yes…terrific reputation.

A Young Waiter comes over and hands them both the menu.

Thank you.

WAITER

A pleasure to see you here, sir.

MAN

Well there you are, darling. The Boeuf En Croute's fantastic.

WAITER

May I recommend today, sir, the Pheasant à la Reine, the sauce is one of the chefs most famous creations.

MAN

Hmmmmm that sounds good…Anyway, darling, you have a look and see what you want. No need to hurry. *(She looks at the menu; he turns casually to the waiter)* Oh by the way…I've got a bit of a dirty fork. Could you possibly get me another one?

WAITER

(incredulously)

I beg your pardon, sir.

MAN

I've got a bit of a dirty fork…Nothing much, but could you get me another one?

WAITER

Oh sir! I do apologize, sir!

MAN

Oh it doesn't worry me – no need to apologize.

WAITER

No, no, sir, I do apologize…I'll fetch the Head Waiter immediately, sir.

MAN

(laughing pleasantly)

Oh no…good heavens – there's no need to do tha…

WAITER

Oh no, sir…I fee sure the Head Waiter will want to apologize personally.
I can't think how it happened. I'll fetch him at once. *(Waiter goes off, leaving the fork on the table)*

LADY

(impressed)

Well, you certainly get good service here.

MAN

Oh yes…they really look after you.

Head Waiter appears closely followed by the Waiter. They both look anxious and tense.

HEAD WAITER

Excuse me sir… *(He picks up the fork)* It's filthy! Who the hell washed this up!
Giuseppe! Find out who washed this up, and give them their cards immediately!

MAN

Er…er…

HEAD WAITER

No no! We can't afford to take any chances! Sack the entire washing-up staff!

MAN

Oh, look please…er…I don't want to cause any trouble.

HEAD WAITER

No, you're quite right to bring this kind of thing to our attention. Giuseppe!
Tell the manager what has happened immediately.

The Waiter runs off.

MAN

Please, I don't want to make a fuss…

HEAD WAITER

There's no fuss, sir. It's simply that we wish to ensure that nothing interferes
with your complete enjoyment of the meal.

MAN

Oh I'm sure it won't…It's only a dirty fork.

HEAD WAITER

I know…and believe me I'm sorry. Bitterly sorry. But I know that no
apologies I can make can alter the fact that in our restaurant you have been
given a dirty, filthy, smelly piece of cutlery!

MAN

It wasn't smelly.

HEAD WAITER

(savagely)

It was smelly, and obscene and disgusting! Oh how I hate it, I hate it!

(The Head Waiter picks up the fork, throws it on the floor and jumps on it. As he is doing this, the Manager appears behind him – his face drawn and anxious.)

MANAGER

(sharply)

That's enough, Gilberto.

HEAD WAITER

Filthy fork! Dirty, smutty, messy, nasty little fork!

MANAGER

Gilberto!

He motions him away with his head. Gilberto leaves mouthing.

Good evening, sir. Good evening, madam. I am the manager, and I…I've only just heard what's happened…May I sit down?

MAN

Yes, yes of course.

MANAGER

I want to apologize, sincerely, humbly and deeply, about the fork.

MAN

Really it was nothing – just a tiny little bit of dirt – you could hardly see it anyway.

MANAGER

Oh you're good, kind, fine people for saying that, but I can see it.
(He stares at fork) To me it's like a boulder…a vast bowl of pus.

MAN

Oh it's not that bad.

Lady looks slightly sick.

MANAGER

No! It gets me…it gets me right here. *(He clenches fist across heart)* I can't give you any excuses for it…there are no excuses. I've wanted to spend more time in the restaurant, but I haven't been too well recently, and we've all been going through a hard time of it, back there…The cook's delinquent son has been put inside again. Poor Mrs. Dalrimple who prepares the salad can hardly move her poor swollen hands…and then of course there's Gilberto's war wound. But they're fine people. And they're good friends, and together we were beginning to get over this bad patch… there was light at the end of the tunnel, when *this*…
(Picks up fork) when *this* happened…

Manager breaks down sobbing at the edge of the table.

MAN

I say look…have some water.

MANAGER

It's the end of the road…*(Blubbers)*

Suddenly an enormous fearful figure brandishing a cleaver looms up behind them…Cringe! Cringe! For it is the mad Cook. Cook stares with hate-filled eyes at the Man.

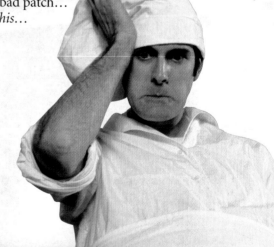

COOK

You bastards!

MAN

I'm sorry?

COOK

You vicious…heartless…bastards!

MAN

Ah…us you mean?

COOK

Look what you've done to him. He's worked his fingers to the bone to make this place what it is…and you come in here with your petty-minded quibbling and you grind him into the dirt! This fine, honourable man! Whose boots you are not worthy to kiss. Oh! It makes me MAD!

Cook whacks the cleaver into the table between the couple.

COOK

Mad!

Gilberto, the Head Waiter, reappears, dragging his leg slightly.

HEAD WAITER

Easy, Mungo. Easy.

COOK

MAD! Stark raving MAD!

HEAD WAITER

Mungo. Ooooh! *(He grabs his leg)* Oh the wound, the wound…

COOK

They've destroyed him.

MANAGER

(suddenly clutching his heart)

No, Mungo. Mungo…*(Dies of heart attack)*

COOK

He's dead. They killed him. *(Cook's eyes take on a more maniac look and he starts wrenching his cleaver out of the table)* Revenge! *(He is about to bring the cleaver down on the couple when the Head Waiter grabs him)*

HEAD WAITER

No, Mungo. Never…kill…a customer. *(He tries to restrain him but gets a fatal attack of the wound and rolls over)* The wound again! *(Dies!)*

At this moment the Young Waiter leaps out of the kitchen and jumps on Mungo. They fight, crashing through the table, breaking everything. Eventually they both lie, dead.

Beat.

Cut to silent film–type caption "And now…the punch line."

MAN

(looking round slightly embarrassed)

Lucky I didn't tell them about the dirty knife!

The Death of Mary, Queen of Scots

RADIO ANNOUNCER

And the naughty bits of Mr. Edward Heath. And that concludes this week's episode of *How to Recognize Different Parts of the Body,* adapted for radio by Ann Haydon-Jones and her husband, Pip. And now we present the first episode of a new radio drama series, *The Death of Mary, Queen of Scots.* Part One, The Beginning.

Theme music. "Coronation Scot."

MAN'S VOICE

You are Mary, Queen of Scots?

WOMAN'S VOICE

I am!

There now follows a series of noises indicating that Mary is getting the shit knocked out of her. Thumps, bangs, slaps, pneumatic drilling, sawing, flogging, shooting, all interlaced with Mary's screams. After a few seconds…

Lay off.

MAN'S VOICE

Take this, Mary Queen of Scots.

The sound effects of violence are redoubled, as is the screaming, but very quickly these sounds fade as the signature tune "Coronation Scot" is brought up loudly to denote the ending of this episode.

RADIO ANNOUNCER

Episode *Two* of *The Death of Mary, Queen of Scots,* can be heard on Radio 4 almost immediately.

Theme music. "Coronation Scot" fading out as sounds of violence and screaming start again and continue unabated in vigor. After a time…

MAN'S VOICE

I think she's dead.

WOMAN'S VOICE

No I'm not.

Sounds of violence and screaming, machine gun fire and explosions start again, rapidly fading under the tune of "Coronation Scot." Mary, Queen of Scots, is just heard to shout "Give over."

RADIO ANNOUNCER

That was Episode Two of *The Death of Mary, Queen of Scots,* adapted for the radio by Bernard Hollowood and Brian London. And now Radio 4 will explode.

Explosion.

Hearing Aid

Smart modern Bond Street optician's shop. Rogers, an assistant, is behind the counter. Door opens and Customer comes in.

CUSTOMER

Good morning. I'm interested in buying a hearing aid.

ROGERS

I'm sorry?

CUSTOMER

I'm interested in buying a hearing aid.

ROGERS

I didn't quite catch it.

CUSTOMER

I want to buy a hearing aid.

ROGERS

Hang on a moment I'll switch the radio off.

He goes to radio and switches very loud music on. His voice is drowned by the music.

Now, sir, what were you saying?

CUSTOMER

What?

ROGERS

What were you saying?

CUSTOMER

I can't hear.

ROGERS

What?

CUSTOMER

The radio's too loud.

ROGERS

Yeah, it's better now isn't it?

Customer switches the radio off.

CUSTOMER

I'm sorry, I couldn't hear what you were saying.

ROGERS

Pardon?…Oh wait a moment, I think my hearing aid's switched off. *(Examines it)* Yes, here we are. Excuse me but I've only had it a few days. Yes, that's better, it's on now.

CUSTOMER

Is it good?

ROGERS
About four guineas.

CUSTOMER
…Yes, but is it good?

ROGERS
No, it fits in the pocket here.

CUSTOMER
Can you hear me?

ROGERS
What?

CUSTOMER
Can you *hear* me?

ROGERS
Oh. Contact lenses.

CUSTOMER
What?

ROGERS
You want contact lenses.

CUSTOMER
No.

ROGERS
I'll get Dr. Waring then because he does the lenses.
(Presses buzzer) I only do the hearing aids.

CUSTOMER
Yes but…

Dr. Waring enters and blinks about him, walks into wall, then wanders over slowly and eventually up to Rogers.

DR. WARING
(to Rogers)

Ah good morning, sir, you want some lenses do you?

ROGERS
What?

DR. WARING
You want some lenses do you?

ROGERS
I can't hear what you're saying, Dr. Waring.

DR. WARING
I think you need a hearing aid, sir, not lenses! Ha, ha.

CUSTOMER
No, I'm the one who wants the hearing aid.

DR. WARING
Who said that? *(Peering around)* Is there someone else here?

ROGERS

What?

DR. WARING

I think there's somebody else here.

CUSTOMER

Yes, it's me. Here.

DR. WARING

Ah now you're the gentleman who wanted the contact lenses.

CUSTOMER

No, I wanted a hearing aid.

DR. WARING

Ah well, Mr. Rogers will deal with that. *(Shouts)* Someone to see you *(To Customer)* He'll be here in a moment. *(To Rogers)* Now *you* wanted the contact lenses did you, sir, come this way.

ROGERS

What?

DR. WARING

(signaling)

This way.

ROGERS

I don't understand. *(They both disappear into Dr. Waring's office)*

Pause. They reappear.

DR. WARING

Why didn't you *say* you were Rogers?

ROGERS

What?

DR. WARING

You know my lenses play me up sometimes. *(He goes up to an empty space)* I do apologize for that confusion. Now you wanted lenses did you?

CUSTOMER

No, I want a hearing aid.

DR. WARING

(to Customer)

Ah, now Mr. Rogers will deal with you, sir. *(Waring then turns back to the empty space)* And I'll deal with this gentleman. Now, sir, if you'd like to come this way. *(He shows the way to his office)* We'll try the lenses. After you…*(He motions in invisible man, enters and closes the door behind him)*

CUSTOMER

Now, Mr. Rogers, I want a hearing aid.

ROGERS

I'm sorry…Look, I'm worried about Dr. Waring. I think he thinks he's with someone.

DR. WARING
(offstage shouting)
Hello! Hello! Hello!

CUSTOMER
Well had you better go and tell him?

ROGERS
No, I'd better go and tell him. *(Opens the door)* Dr. Waring!

DR. WARING
Ah, there you are. I thought I'd lost you.

ROGERS
Dr. Waring, you're not with anybody.

DR. WARING
Well, who's that talking to me? Don't be silly. Sit down. *(Closes the door)*

ROGERS
What? *(Door is closed)*

Pause. Door opens. They reappear.

DR. WARING
Well, why didn't you *say* you were Rogers?

ROGERS
It's a quarter past four.

Waring goes up to another empty space.

DR. WARING
Now, are you the gentleman who wanted the contact lenses?

CUSTOMER
No, I wanted the hearing aid!

DR. WARING
(to Customer)

So you must want the contact lenses.

CUSTOMER
I want a hearing aid!

DR. WARING
Ah, these two gentlemen want a hearing aid, Rogers.

ROGERS
What? Hang on, I can't hear. I think it must be this hearing aid. Hang on.
(He hits it, Sound FX – very high pitched whine) Oh, ow. Help, it's so loud it hurts.
(Beats the hearing aid in agony, then gives it an extra hard bang, silence) Ah,
that's better. Oh, wait a moment I've knocked my contact lenses out. Don't move.

Rogers starts groveling about on the floor feeling for them.
Shop door opens and a Second Customer enters. He is in a mess.

CUSTOMER 2
(Shouting) I want to complain about my contact lenses.

DR. WARING

(surprised)

What?

CUSTOMER 2

I want to complain about my contact lenses. They're terrible. They've ruined my eyesight.

DR. WARING

(to Original Customer)

I haven't given you any.

CUSTOMER 2

You're a liar.

DR. WARING

What?

CUSTOMER 2

You swindler, you money-grubbing quack.

DR. WARING

(still to Original Customer)

Don't you speak to me like that.

CUSTOMER 2

I'll speak to you how I want. *(Walks into wall)* Oh fisticuffs!

DR. WARING

What?

CUSTOMER 2

Rough stuff, eh?

DR. WARING

If that's the way you want it.

CUSTOMER

Keep away from me.

DR. WARING

Ah backing out now are you?

CUSTOMER 2

Take that! *(Punches bookshelf)*

DR. WARING

Missed! Ha, ha, too quick for you.

CUSTOMER 2

Had enough?

DR. WARING

NO. *(Swings punch at the same time as Customer 2 walks into a lamp)*

Chaos.

– Blackout –

Ken Shabby

ROSAMUND

Daddy, the man I love is here.

FATHER

All right, send him in.

ROSAMUND

Come, Ken.

Ken Shabby enters. He is very shabby indeed with an old torn coat and a beret.

FATHER

I believe you want to marry my daughter?

KEN SHABBY

(sniffing and coughing)

That's right…yeah…yeah…

FATHER

You realize of course that Rosamund is still rather young?

KEN SHABBY

(lasciviously)

Yeah…oooh…yeah…rather…get 'em young eh…eh…OOOH!

Shabby makes an obscene gesture involving his elbow.

ROSAMUND

Father, you make me feel like a child.

FATHER

Well I'm sure you know what I mean, Mr…?

KEN SHABBY

Shabby…Ken Shabby…

FATHER

Mr. Shabby…I want to make sure you can look after Rosamund.

KEN SHABBY

Don't worry about that…sport…I'll look after her all right…Eurggh!

FATHER

What job do you do?

KEN SHABBY

I clean out public conveniences.

FATHER

Is there promotion involved?

KEN SHABBY

Oh yeah, yeah. *(Produces handkerchief and gobs horribly into it)* After five years they give me a brush…eurggha…eurgh…Oh sorry, I've gobbed on your carpet…

FATHER

Where are you going to live?

KEN SHABBY

Round at my Gran's…She trains polecats, but half of them have died so she's got a bit of spare room in the attic.

FATHER

And when are you thinking of getting married?

KEN SHABBY

Right away…No hangin' about, guvnor…Know what I mean…I haven't had it for weeks…nudge nudge…eh.

FATHER

Well, I'll ring the bishop and see if we can get the abbey…

KEN SHABBY

Oh, shit. *(Coughing fit)*

FATHER

Right, stop it there.

ROSAMUND

What do you mean, Father?

FATHER

(putting Colonel's hat on)

I'm stopping this sketch.

KEN SHABBY

You can't do that.

FATHER

I'm the senior officer here and I haven't had a single funny line so I *am* stopping it.

ROSAMUND

Meanie.

FATHER

Shut up. Now let's have a nice simple sketch with none of this unpleasantness – something with John Cleese in it. He's not normally dirty. How about a Michael Miles take-off. They always go well.

189

Michael Miles Game Show

A simple quiz game set with a typical grinning host.

MICHAEL MILES

And could we have the next contestant please?

A Pepperpot walks out towards Michael Miles.

MICHAEL MILES

Good evening, madam, and what is your name?

PEPPERPOT

I go to church regularly.

MICHAEL MILES

And what prize do you have your eyes on this evening?

PEPPERPOT

I'd like the blow on the head.

MICHAEL MILES

The blow on the head!

PEPPERPOT

(pointing)

Just there.

MICHAEL MILES

Jolly good. Well your first question for a blow on the head is "Which great opponent of Cartesian rationalism resists the reduction of all psychological phenomena to physical states and insists that there is no point of contact between the unextended and the extended?"

PEPPERPOT

Oooh, I don't know that.

MICHAEL MILES

Have a guess.

PEPPERPOT

Henri Bergson?

MICHAEL MILES

Is correct.

PEPPERPOT

Oh, that was lucky, I never even heard of him.

MICHAEL MILES

Jolly good.

PEPPERPOT

I don't like darkies.

MICHAEL MILES

Your second question is "What is the principal food that penguins eat?"

PEPPERPOT

Pork luncheon meat.

190

MICHAEL MILES

No.

PEPPERPOT

Spam?

MICHAEL MILES

No, penguins. *What* do penguins eat?

PEPPERPOT

Other penguins?

MICHAEL MILES

No.

PEPPERPOT

Armchairs.

MICHAEL MILES

No, no, no.

PEPPERPOT

Sofas.

MICHAEL MILES

No, no, what do penguins eat?

PEPPERPOT

Oh, penguins. Cannelloni.

MICHAEL MILES

No.

PEPPERPOT

Lasagna, Fettuccini a la Vongole, Moussaka, Sauté de Beouf a la Provençale, Lobster Lily Langtry, Escalopes de Veau a l'Estragon avec Pommes Duchesses and Endives Gratinéed with cheese.

MICHAEL MILES

No, no, no, no.

PEPPERPOT

Ah! George Bush.

MICHAEL MILES

No.

PEPPERPOT

George Washington? George the Third? George Lucas?

MICHAEL MILES

No no!

PEPPERPOT

Luke Skywalker!

MICHAEL MILES

No. What swims in the sea and gets caught in nets?

PEPPERPOT

Henri Bergson.

MICHAEL MILES

No.

PEPPERPOT

Goats. Underwater goats with snorkels and flippers.

MICHAEL MILES

No no.

PEPPERPOT

A buffalo with an aqualung.

MICHAEL MILES

No no.

PEPPERPOT

Reginald Maudling.

MICHAEL MILES

Yes, I'll give you that. That's near enough. Right, now you've won your prize. Do you still want a blow on the head?

PEPPERPOT

Yes please.

MICHAEL MILES

I'll offer you a poke in the eye.

No! Blow on the head.

MICHAEL MILES

A punch in the throat.

PEPPERPOT

No.

MICHAEL MILES

A kick on the kneecap?

PEPPERPOT

No.

MICHAEL MILES

All right then, a foot in the teeth and a dagger up the strap.

PEPPERPOT

Er…

Chorus of Pepperpots shout out of vision: "Take the blow on the head."

PEPPERPOT

No, no. I'll take the blow on the head.

MICHAEL MILES

Very well, you have won…the blow on the head.

He strikes her on the head and she falls down unconscious.

Minister Falling to Pieces

TV interview with Minister behind desk.

INTERVIEWER

We're lucky to have here in the studio this evening Mr. James Pemberton, the minister of fuel. Good evening, Minister.

MINISTER

Good evening.

INTERVIEWER

Minister, you've been in Germany this week studying new coal face methods, do you think you've learned much that will be of help to British coal production?

MINISTER

Well it's very difficult to say at this stage but it does look as though…

A loud clang.

…Good heavens. My foot's dropped off.

INTERVIEWER

Gone to sleep, Minister?

MINISTER

No, it's dropped off. My foot's dropped off. Look there it is under the table. It…fell off.

INTERVIEWER

Well will it screw back on?

MINISTER

Of course it won't screw back on. Your foot doesn't screw back on does it?

INTERVIEWER

Er, could we have the camera round on the minister's foot, please?

MINISTER

Keep the bloody camera away from my foot. I don't want people staring at it.

INTERVIEWER

But, Minister, how did it drop off?

MINISTER

I don't know, it's never happened before. It just fell off.
(Another clang)
There goes the other one. My feet have dropped off. Both of them.
(Another clang)

INTERVIEWER

Oh dear the Minister's falling to pieces.

MINISTER

(sinking behind the desk)
Why did this have to happen on television?

INTERVIEWER

Would somebody get a box? Minister, how do you feel about falling to pieces?

Somebody brings a box in. Clangs ad-lib until the end.

MINISTER

Oh my thigh. My thigh's fallen off.

INTERVIEWER

(bending down)

Is this your knee?

MINISTER

Of course it's my knee. Whose do you think it is? Put it in the box.

INTERVIEWER

(changing subject)

We'd like to move on now to an item that's right in the news today…

MINISTER

I'm falling to pieces, help!

INTERVIEWER

Sugar beet farming in East Anglia…

MINISTER

(disappearing under desk)

Put me in the box and for God's sake don't lose any of the bits.

INTERVIEWER

Good night, Minister.

Man collecting the pieces eventually goes off with a boxful of Minister.

Secret Service

Man A is crouching under a desk as Man B is entering.

MAN A

(appearing from behind desk)
Ah, Mr. Leighton, do come in, make yourself at home. Good.
(Man sits) So you're interested in joining the Secret Service, are you?

MAN B

Yes.

MAN A

Splendid – now in this branch we need alert, intelligent, active men with good nerves – you have got good nerves, have you?

MAN B

Yes, I think so.

MAN A

Good. They're absolutely essential in the type of work we're…*(Phone rings. He almost leaps out of his skin.)* Ah, yes, Miss Jackson – will you bring Mr. Leighton's file please. Thank you.
(Replaces phone) Sorry to keep you waiting. Won't be a moment.

A tall man enters with a file and puts it on the desk.

Thank you, Miss Jackson. Wait a minute. *You're* not Miss Jackson.

The Man camps a little.

Oh, yes you are. Good disguise, Miss Jackson. Well done…Oh, one thing before you go, what did you do with the big file that was on my desk here yesterday, the one marked "Top Highly Secret" about all that nuclear nonsense?

MISS JACKSON

I gave it to that foreign-looking gentlemen who called yesterday, sir.

MAN A

(shouting at Miss Jackson)
DO YOU PLAY CRICKET?
(conversationally to Man B) You're fired.
(double-takes) I'm sorry.
(Shouting after the retreating Miss Jackson) YOU'RE FIRED!
(Conversationally to Man B) Do you play cricket?

MAN B

No, I play tennis.

MAN A

Oh, I used to play cricket. I remember on one occasion I was bowling to one fellow, ex–county player he was actually. *(Illustrates the rest of cricket story with gestures)* I gave him a half volley just outside the off-stump. He put his foot down the wicket. Hit the ball back at me like a bullet. Never had a chance to move. Ball hit me plum between the eyes…

He passes out and slumps backwards into his chair. Pause. Comes round slowly and resumes normal seated position.

I gave him a half volley outside the off-stump, he put his foot down the wicket. Hit the ball back at me like a bullet. Never had a chance to move. Ball hit me…*(Collapses again, recovers)* Where was I?

MAN B

Bowling.

MAN A

Ah, yes. I gave him a shorter, faster one. He went on the back foot, hit the ball back at me like a bullet. Never had a chance to move. Over my shoulder. Down to the sight screen. Fielder ran round, picked the ball up, threw it in. I was watching the wicket keeper. Ball landed right on the back bbbbbbbb… *(Collapses third time, recovers)* Last ball of the over, I gave him a slower one. Threw the ball right up into the air. He came down the wicket, took the ball on the full toss, hit it back at me like a bullet. Never had a chance to move. Couldn't protect myself. Ball hit me straight smack plum between the eyes.

B anticipates disaster. Nothing happens.

Of course, I was getting used to it by then. Now what languages do you speak? French?

MAN B

Yes.

MAN A

German? Sprechen Sie Deutsch?

MAN B

Ya, ich spreche ein weinige Deutsch ich kant auf diese wiese eine billiger lachen bekommen.

MAN A

You're not German are you?

MAN B

No.

MAN A

Good, good. Now do you think you could take pain? Do you think you could put up with physical torture?

MAN B

Oh I hope so, yes.

MAN A

Good. I had five years in a Jap camp you know. Or was is Malayan – No, Japanese. *(His left hand does a convulsive shake)* Yes, nasty experience. *(Convulsion repeated)* Got over it though. *(His right hand runs after his left hand, catches it and brings it back, smacks it, lifts it up and puts a pen in it and puts it down.)* Now let's just have a look at your record: Oxford, first in modern languages. Tennis blue, play the piano, mandolin…You're not Chinese, are you?

MAN B

No.

MAN A

Good, we don't want them in the Secret Service. They're not as bad as the Japs though…*(Pointing)* They come over the filing cabinet there after the strawberries. Do you want a strawberry? *(Realizes he is having a turn and goes into stuttering routine)* Why do you want to join why do you want to join why do you want to join the Secret Service?

MAN B

Well, I…

MAN A

Why do you want to join the Secret Service?

MAN B

Well, I…

MAN A

Can you keep a secret?

MAN B

Yes, I think so.

MAN A

Good. You're in then.

Goes into frantic scribbling routine as Man B tries unsuccessfully to see what he is writing.

Now, any good at codes?

MAN B

No, I'm afraid not.

MAN A

Doesn't matter, doesn't matter. What would you say to the purple wombat claps its feet?

MAN B

I'm afraid I've no idea.

MAN A

Have a go.

MAN B

But I've absolutely no idea.

MAN A

Don't be wet, man, have a go.

MAN B

Oh, all right…The walls of Jericho are slimy green.

MAN A

Quite right. Well done. Now, coffee?

MAN B

Yes please.

Man A picks up a nonexistent phone.

MAN A

Hello, could we have two of those delicious coffees please.

He realizes the phone is non-existent and picks up the real one.

Hello, two coffees, please. Yes, cancel the other two.

He replaces the phone.

There's someone behind you.

B turns, A laughs at him, then turns around in fright and then recovers.

Now, one small thing I noticed, your name: Obolenskovitchsky. You're not Russian, are you?

MAN B

Yes.

MAN A

You *are* a Russian?

MAN B

Yes.

MAN A

Well, that's no good We don't want Russians in the Secret Service. It wouldn't be secret. Out you go then.

Man B draws revolver from pocket.

MAN B

Smith and Wesson 42. Cattle pin holster file. You know they were first brought out in 1962…

Man B fires. Beat.

MAN A

Now…the reason that I know that that was a blank that you fired then was that there was practically no kick.

Throughout speech A notices by feeling his chest and then tasting blood on his fingers that he has a real bullet wound.

Did you notice that? And the other thing was, you see the smoke that came out of the barrel was grayish in color. If you fire a real bullet you get a bluish tinge, round the outside of the flame. It's the sort of thing you pick up when you've been in the department for a year or two. *(He picks up his phone)* Would you make that just one coffee please?

He dies.

– Blackout –

Cocktail Bar

Pub sign "The Fox and Half-A-Bee." Fairly plush cocktail-type bar. Cheerful Barman at work. Three City-Type Gents approach bar.

CITY GENT 1

So he switched into tin, moved his lead assets into copper, got the rest of the family into vanadium, except for the half-sister who was obsessed with zinc, financed the coup, sold the bodies, made a quick turnover and got into Angel cakes.

CITY GENT 2

Which is where he went wrong.

CITY GENT 3

Exactly.

CITY GENT 2

When's the funeral?

CITY GENT 1

He hasn't killed himself yet.

CITY GENT 2

He hasn't?

CITY GENT 1

No he's waiting till April 5.

CITY GENT 3

Some sort of tax dodge.

BARMAN

Good evening, sir.

All together.

CITY GENT 1

Good evening, Tom.

CITY GENT 2

Good evening, Harry.

CITY GENT 3

Good evening, Jim.

BARMAN

What's it going to be sir?

Buzz from counter. He swats it with his paper.

CITY GENT 1

(to City Gent 2)

Mark?

CITY GENT 2

One of your specials, Harry.

CITY GENT 1

One special, Tom.

BARMAN

Certainly, sir. *(Pours out cocktail standing by)* Twist of lemming, sir?

CITY GENT 2

Please, Harry.

BARMAN

(Squeezing lemming's neck into glass, it squeaks)

Bit more, sir?

CITY GENT 2

Just a drop.

BARMAN

(Squeezing lemming again, another squeal, he throws it in bin)

There you are, sir.

CITY GENT 1

(to City Gent 3)

Alex?

CITY GENT 3

Mallard Fizz please, Jim.

CITY GENT 2

Hear about old Guy Barclay?

CITY GENT 3

What?

CITY GENT 2

Gone into cork. *Was* in tinsel, switched via wood preservatives into entrails, financed the coup, took up his option on the bodies, cornered the market.

CITY GENT 1

Good luck to him.

During this time the Barman has taken the cocktail shaker, added Angostura and vodka, then taken a mallard duck, tried it for size, taken a cleaver, cleaved its head off and put the head in the shaker followed by an egg and Tabasco sauce. He shakes it frantically.

CITY GENT 2

Smart fellow. Thought he'd do well, nice close eyes and virtually no earlobes and a bank balance as big as your foot.

CITY GENT 3

Got funny elbows too, bend the wrong way.

CITY GENT 1

Really?

CITY GENT 3

Had two years in the army, every time he saluted people fainted. Don't wait for me, Mark.

CITY GENT 2

Oh thanks, cheers. *(Knocks it back in one, goes pale)* Excuse me.
(Runs off to vomit)

By now City Gent 3 is getting his Mallard Fizz. Barman garnishes it with the duck's head.

BARMAN

There you are, sir.

CITY GENT 3

Thanks, Jim. *(Not drinking it yet)*

CITY GENT 1

Harlem Stinger, Tom.

BARMAN

Yes sir. Rastus! *(Calling off, big black man arrives)*

RASTUS

Yes, boss.

BARMAN

One Stinger please.

RASTUS

One Stinger coming up.

Rastus opens mouth, Barman pours a couple of bottles in, adds a couple of extras, Rastus gargles for several seconds then spits it out into glass, Barman picks it up and hands it to City Gent 1.

CITY GENT 3

Cheers. *(Swallows drink, reacts, disappears sickly)*

CITY GENT 1

How much is that then?

BARMAN

£1.40, sir.

CITY GENT 1

Would you care to join us?

BARMAN

No thank you, sir. *(Takes money)*

CITY GENT 1

Cheers. *(Swallows, runs to loo door, can't get in, runs to waste paper basket, vomits. At this moment City Gent 2 reappears from the loo white and shaken, totters to bar and gets on stool, head in hands)*

CITY GENT 2

Same again, Harry, oh Christ!

Barman pours out cocktail, takes out a lemming.

Easy on the lemming, Harry.

BARMAN

Certainly, sir. *(Squeak squeak)*

City Gent 3 comes back.

Same again for you, sir?

CITY GENT 3

Just a small one.

CITY GENT 2

(looking at drink)

Harry.

BARMAN

Yes, sir.

CITY GENT 2

Have you got something a bit lighter?

BARMAN

Something without the mallard sir?

CITY GENT 2

Yes, please, Harry.

BARMAN

How about a Safari Snowball?

CITY GENT 2

That's more like it.

Barman produces a gun and leaves.

BARMAN

Won't be a moment, sir.

202

Undertaker

Undertaker is on stage. Man enters.

UNDERTAKER

Hallo!

MAN

Good morning.

UNDERTAKER

What can I do for you, squire?

MAN

Well I wonder if you can help me…My mother has just died and I'm not quite sure what to do.

UNDERTAKER

Oh well we can help you. We deal with stiffs.

MAN

Stiffs?

UNDERTAKER

Yeah, there's three things we can do with your mum. We can bury her, burn her or dump her.

MAN

Dump her?

UNDERTAKER

Dump her in the Thames?

MAN

What?

UNDERTAKER

Oh did you like her?

MAN

Yes.

UNDERTAKER

Oh well we won't dump her then. Well what do you think? A burner or a burier.

MAN

Well which do you recommend?

UNDERTAKER

Well, they're both nasty…With a burner, we stuff her in the fire, and she goes up in smoke, bit of a shock if she's not quite dead, but quick, and then we give you a box of ashes, which you can pretend are hers.

MAN

Oh.

UNDERTAKER

Or if you don't want to fry her, we can bury her and then she'll get eaten up by maggots and weevils, which isn't so hot if, as I said, she's not quite dead.

MAN

I see. Well I'm sure she's definitely dead.

UNDERTAKER

Where is she?

MAN

She's in this sack.

UNDERTAKER

Let's have a look. *(Looks)* Oh! She looks quite young.

MAN

Yes she was.

UNDERTAKER

Fred!

FRED

(putting head round the inside door)

Yeh?

UNDERTAKER

I think we've got an eater.

MAN

What?

FRED

I'll put the oven on.

MAN

I'm sorry but are you suggesting we should eat my mother?

UNDERTAKER

Er…yeah, not raw! Cooked.

MAN

What?

UNDERTAKER

Yes…roasted with a few French fries and some broccoli. Smashing.

MAN

Well I do feel a bit peckish.

UNDERTAKER

Great!

MAN

Can we have some parsnips?

UNDERTAKER

Put some parsnips on. How about stuffing?

MAN

No, no, wait a moment. I really don't think I should.

UNDERTAKER

Look. We'll eat her and then if you feel a bit guilty about it after, we'll dig a trench and you can throw up in it.

Blackmail

Music up - wild applause and cheers from the audience. Spotlight up on the word "Blackmail" in letters 4 feet high, picked out in light bulbs, which flash on and off.

Presenter in glittery showbiz jacket sits behind glittery desk.

PRESENTER
Hallo and welcome to *Blackmail*! And to start today's show, let's see our first contestant on the big screen please: Mrs. Betty Teal!

On the screen comes up a slightly blurred black and white photo of a housewife with her face blotted out by a black oblong.

Hallo, Mrs. Teal! *(He picks up a letter and reads it)* Now this is for Mrs. Teal, if you're looking in tonight, this is for fifteen pounds and it's to stop us revealing the name of your lover in Bolton…

A slide reads "£15," which flashes on and off the screen quickly.

So Mrs. Teal…if you're looking in tonight send us fifteen pounds before next week and your husband Trevor, and your lovely children Diane, Janice, and Juliet, need never know the name…of your lover in Bolton.

Spotlight up on Naughty Organist who is sitting back to the audience at a small organ on far side of stage. He wears a full evening dress, with a hole cut out of the back revealing his bare buttocks. He plays a few stirring chords.

Thank you, Onan! *(As he speaks he holds up the various items)* Now…a letter… a hotel registration book…and a series of photographs…which could add up to divorce, premature retirement, and possible criminal proceedings for a company director in Bromsgrove. He's head of a Printing Works, he's a Freemason, and a prospective Tory M.P.…that's Mr. S of Bromsgrove…three thousand pounds…*(Super "£3,000" flashes and off)*…to stop us revealing your name…the name of the three other people involved, the youth organization to which they belonged, and the shop where you bought the equipment!

Spotlight on Naughty Organist with chords again.

Thank you and now let's have our second photo please!

On-screen still of two pairs of naked feet and lower legs. Organ music plays over this.

And we'll be showing more of that photograph later in the programme unless we hear from Charles or Michael. And now it's time for the moment you've all been waiting for – our *Stop The Film* spot!

Gay sparkling caption on screen "Stop The Film." Cheery zippy music plays.
Lady in spangled outfit, with black strip of cardboard masking out her eyes (as in Mrs. Teal's photo) brings on the glittering phone and places it on the desk.

Thank you…Dan…Now the rules are very simple. We have taken a film which contains compromising scenes and unpleasant details, which could wreck a man's career. But, the victim may phone me whilst the film is being shown, and stop it at any point. But don't forget, the money increases as the film goes on. So the longer you leave it…the more you have to pay! This week, *Stop The Film* visited Thames Ditton.

As the film progresses we have a £ sign with numerals in one corner - which increase.

Film of a residential street in Thames Ditton.

Another section of a street with a figure in a Robin Hood hat and raincoat in distance on far side of road so we can't really make him out.

Cut to slightly closer shot of him about to cross the road (taken from the other side with cars flashing in front of camera, which is hand held).

Cut to suburban house. The Man is standing at the door pressing the bell and looking round rather furtively. Again shot from some distance and over a hedge. Perhaps with shaky zoom-ins.Presenter looking at screen and then at the phone.

        Isn't this fun…!

We are looking at the doorway still. A Woman opening the door. She wears a dressing gown over lingerie, again with a shaky zoom in to reveal her clothing.
Wide shot of house with door shut.
Jump cut to shot obviously taken from a window in the house. Shaky zoom in on window. We can see the window. Both the Man and the Woman enter the bedroom. He goes out of shot, taking his coat off.

        He's a very brave man…

Even closer perhaps on window. Series of short jump cuts.
She is undressing.
Throws off her dressing gown.
Jump cut and she's taking off her negligee.
Jump cut and underneath she wears black corsets.
She produces a whip and seems to be beckoning the man.
Sound F/X of phone ringing on desk.
Presenter picks up the phone.

        Hello…Hello, sir?…Yes…I'm sure you didn't, sir…It's all right, sir, we don't morally censor, we just want the money…by tomorrow morning. Well, that was exciting. Remember if you find yourself playing *Stop The Film*, here's the address to send the money to:

Caption comes up on screen:
"Blackmail
Behind the Hot Water Pipes
Third Washroom Along
Victoria Station"

        (*Into phone*) Not at all, thank *you*, sir. (*Replaces phone*) Well we'll be back at the same time next week…when we'll be playing *Pederasto* – the game for all the family. See you then.

Music, F/X of recorded applause…

The Presenter walks off and he has no trousers on.

Pause.

Then a Woman appears from beneath his desk and runs off after him.

        – Blackout –

Courtroom

A courtroom. Various dummies or cut-outs sit in the jury box.

JUDGE

Michael Norman Randall, you have been found guilty of the murder of the Right Reverend Arthur Claude Webster, Bishop of Leicester, Charles Patrick Trumpington, Bishop of Birmingham, Ronald Victor Harmsworth, Bishop of Leeds, Prebendary Charles MacIntyre Potter, Moderator of the Church of Scotland, Reverend Nigel Sinclair Robinson, Reverend John Claude Motson, Father Kevin Joyce O'Malley, Dean Robert William Palmer, Monsignor Jean-Paul Reynard, Padre Robert Henry Noonan, Rabbi Edwin Makepeace Goodgold, Pope Pius Mario Vercotti, Pastor Karl-Heinz Biolek, Archbishop Stavros Nicolas Parsons, His Most Holy and Indivisible Oneness Hwang Ky Sung and Raj Arthur Buddha, on or about the morning of the third Sunday in Epiphany. Have you anything to say before this court considers your case and passes sentence upon you?

RANDALL

Yes sir, I'm very sorry. It was a very bad thing to have done and I'm really very ashamed of myself. I can only say it won't happen again. I really feel…

JUDGE

Oh shut up! How do you plead?

Randall holds two fingers up and demonstrates to court à la charades.

Two words…

Randall nods. Holds up one finger.

First word…

Randall does tying-up-a-tie mime.
Various "ers" and furrowed brows from the rest of the court.

Er…tie…er knot…Knot!

Randall thumbs-up then does fish mime.

Er…swim…er…fish…fish! Knot fishy…

Randall shakes head and exaggerates fish mime and points to his neck.

Knot Gill…er…Tie!

Randall nods.

Knot Gill Tie! The defendant has pleaded Knot Gill Tie.

Applause from court.

Okay, Mr. Smith for the prosecution.

TYPIST

Sorry? How do you…

JUDGE

What?

TYPIST

How do you spell that? S…M…I…then I go a bit wrong.

JUDGE

T. H.

TYPIST

Oh! Of course, S…M…I…T…H…

JUDGE

Right, carry on.

SMITH

Your Honour –

TYPIST

Sorry…

JUDGE

What?

TYPIST

What did you say before Smith?

JUDGE

Oh just get down what you can…

Policeman gets up.

POLICEMAN

May I ask for an adjournment?

JUDGE

An adjournment…certainly not!

Policeman sits down. There is a loud fart. P.C. goes bright red.

Why didn't you say *why* you wanted an adjournment?

POLICEMAN

I didn't know an acceptable legal phrase.

JUDGE

You may be adjourned, Constable.

POLICEMAN

(as he goes)

You won't all listen?

JUDGE

Mr. Smith for the prosecution.

SMITH

Sir, we all know the facts of the case; that Sapper Walters being in charge of expensive military equipment to wit one Lee Enfield 303 rifle and seventy-two

rounds of ammunition, valued at £140.3/6, chose instead to use wet towels to take an enemy command post in the area of Basingstoke…

JUDGE

Basingstoke? Basingstoke in Hampshire?

SMITH

No, no, no, sir.

JUDGE

I see, carry on then.

SMITH

The result of Sapper Walters's action was that the enemy…

JUDGE

Basingstoke *where*?

SMITH

Basingstoke in Westphalia, sir.

JUDGE

I see, carry on.

SMITH

The result of the action was that the enemy got wet patches on their uniforms and in some cases little red marks on their thighs and on…

JUDGE

I didn't know there *was* a Basingstoke in Westphalia.

SMITH

(slightly irritably)

It's on the map, sir.

JUDGE

What map?

SMITH

(more irritably)

The map of Westphalia as used by the army, sir.

JUDGE

Well I certainly never heard of a Basingstoke in Westphalia.

SMITH

(patiently)

It's a municipal borough, sir, twenty-seven miles N.N.E. of Southampton, its chief manufactures are leather…

JUDGE

What…Southampton in Westphalia?

SMITH

Yes, sir…agricultural implements…bricks…clothing. Nearby are the remains of Basing House, burned down in 1645 by Cromwell's forces after a two-year siege.

JUDGE

Who compiled this map?

SMITH

Cole Porter, sir.

JUDGE

(incredulously)

Cole Porter…who wrote *Kiss Me Kate*?

SMITH

No, alas not, sir…this is the Cole Porter who wrote *Anything Goes*…
Anyway, I shall seek to prove that the man before this court…

JUDGE

That's the same one! *(He sings)* "In olden days a glimpse of stocking…"

SMITH

I *beg* your pardon, sir?

JUDGE

(singing)

"In olden days a glimpse of stocking was looked on as something shocking,
Now heaven knows, Anything goes…"

SMITH

Ah no, this one's different, sir.

JUDGE

How does it go?

SMITH

What, sir?

JUDGE

How does *your* "Anything Goes" go?

WALTERS

Can I go home?

JUDGE

Shut up! *(To Smith)* Come on!

SMITH

Really sir, this is rather…

JUDGE

Come on, how does your "Anything Goes" go?

SMITH

(clearing throat and going into extraordinarily tuneless and very loud song)

Anything goes in. Anything goes out!
Fish, bananas, old pajamas,
Mutton! Beef! and trout!
Anything goes in!
Anything…

JUDGE

No, that's not it…Carry on.

SMITH

With respect, sir, I shall seek to prove that Sapper Walters, being in possession of the following…one pair of boots, value £3.7/6, one pair of serge trousers, value £2.3/6, one pair of gaiters value £68.10/-, one…

JUDGE

£68.10/- for a pair of *gaiters*?

SMITH

(dismissively)

They were special gaiters, sir.

JUDGE

Special gaiters?

SMITH

Yes, they were made in France. One beret costing 14 shillings, one pair of…

POLICEMAN

What was so special about them?

SMITH

(dismissively)

Oh…*(As if he can hardly be bothered to reply)* they were made of special fabric. The buckles were made of empire silver instead of brass. The total value of the uniform was there…

POLICEMAN

Why was he wearing special gaiters?

SMITH

(getting irritated)

They were a presentation pair, from the Regiment, sir. The total value of the…

JUDGE

Why did they present him with a special pair of gaiters?

SMITH

Sir I hardly feel it is relevant to the case…whether his gaiters were presented or not.

JUDGE

I think the court will be able to judge that for themselves. *Why* did the Regiment present the accused with a special pair of gaiters?

SMITH

(stifling his impatience)

…He…used to do things for them. The total value…

JUDGE

What things?

SMITH

(*exasperated*)

He…he used to oblige them, sir.

JUDGE

Oblige them?

SMITH

Yes, sir. The *total value* of the entire…

JUDGE

How did he oblige them?

SMITH

What sir?

JUDGE

How did he *oblige* them?

SMITH

(*more and more irritated*)

He made them…he made them happy in little ways, sir. The value could therefore not have been *less* than…

JUDGE

Did he touch them at all?

SMITH

Sir! I submit this is totally irrelevant.

JUDGE

I want to know how he made them happy.

SMITH

(*suddenly losing patience*)

He used to ram things up their…!

JUDGE

(*quickly*)

All right! All right! No need to *spell* it out! (*Rather at a loss*) What, er, what does the…er…prisoner have to say?

WALTERS

(*taken off guard*)

What me?

JUDGE

Yes, what have you got to say?

WALTERS

What can I say, sir? How can I encapsulate in mere words my scorn for any military solution? The futility of modern warfare? And the hypocrisy by which the contemporary government applies one standard to violence perpetrated by one community upon another and another to violence perpetrated by individuals? How indeed could…

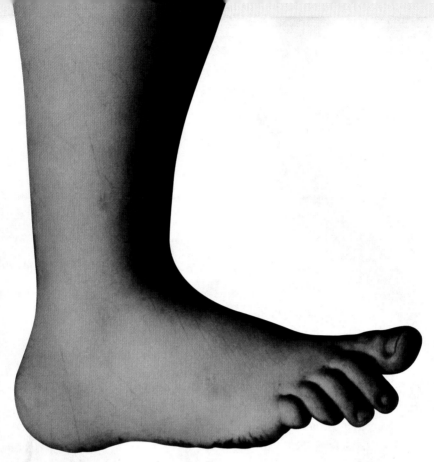

At this point the Defence Counsel enters.

DEFENCE

I'm sorry, m'lud, my client has become pretentious. And I'm sorry I'm late, I couldn't find a kosher car park.

POLICEMAN

(stands up again; he's obviously in some discomfort)
Your Honour…Could I…

JUDGE

What? Not again?

DEFENCE

Call Mrs. Fiona Lewis…

Enter a Garrulous Lady.

FIONA

I swear to tell the truth, the whole truth and nothing but the truth so anyway, I said to her I said "That Mrs. Harris at number four!" She's the one that had the new bin last week, the bony woman with the new carpet, you know, four by twelve with green marks that looks just like a dead crab you know, well anyway I said they can't afford that on what he earns, I mean for a start the feathers get up your nose, I ask you four and six a pound, and him with a wooden leg, I don't know how she puts up with it what with all the trouble she's had with her you know what, anyway it was a white wedding much to everyone's surprise, course it's all on the hire purchase you know, they ought to send them back where they come from, you've got to be cruel to be kind so Mrs. Harris said, she said she said, so she said she said, well her sister's gone to Rhodesia what with her womb and their youngest being as thin as a filing cabinet, well the goldfish has whooping cough and kept spitting water all over their Hockney's well they do don't they I mean you can't, can you, they're not married or anything, they're not even divorced and he's in the KGB if you ask me, says he's a tree surgeon but I don't like the sound of his liver, all that squeaking and banging every night till the small hours, they ought to send them to the Martin Heidegger Institute in Baden Baden, I mean his mother's been less trouble since she had her head off, so I said "Don't you talk to me about bladders" so she…

During all this, Defence Counsel has been trying to ask questions. He eventually gives up and Mrs. Lewis is carried out of the court still talking.

JUDGE
Mr. Bartlett, I don't see the relevance of your last witness.

DEFENCE
I think my next witness will explain that if m'ludship will allow.
Call the late Arthur Aldridge.

JUDGE
The *late* Arthur Aldridge?

DEFENCE
Yes, m'lud.

A coffin is brought into the court and laid across the witness box.

JUDGE
Mr. Bartlett, do you think there is any point in questioning the deceased?

DEFENCE
I beg your pardon, m'lud?

JUDGE
Er, well…your witness is dead?

DEFENCE
Yes, m'lud. Well, virtually, m'lud. Mr. Aldridge…

JUDGE
He's not completely dead?

DEFENCE

No he's not completely dead, m'lud. But he's not at all well.

JUDGE

But if he's not dead, why's he in a coffin?

DEFENCE

It's just a precaution, m'lud. If I may continue, Mr. Aldridge, you were a…you *are* a stockbroker of 10 Sevona Close Wimbledon.

From the coffin comes a BANG!

JUDGE

What was that knock?

DEFENCE

It means "Yes," m'lud. One knock for "Yes," two for "No." Mr. Aldridge, would it be fair to say that you are not very well?

From the coffin comes a BANG!

In fact, Mr. Aldridge, not to put too fine a point on it, would you be prepared to say that you are, as it were, in a manner of speaking, what is commonly known as *dead*?

Silence. Defence Counsel listens.

I think he's dead, m'lud.

JUDGE

Where is all this leading?

DEFENCE

That will become apparent in a moment, m'lud. *(Walking over to the coffin)* Of course, he may just be thinking. Mr. Aldridge, are you thinking or are you just dead? *(Long pause)* I think I'd better have a look, m'lud. *(He opens the coffin and looks inside for some time, then he closes the coffin)* No further questions, m'lud.

JUDGE

What do you mean "No further questions"? You can't just dump dead bodies in my court and say "No further questions." Does the prosecution have any witnesses?

PROSECUTION

I have just one witness sir…Call Police Constable Pan-Am…

P.C. Pan-Am runs into court and starts to assault Randall violently with his truncheon.

JUDGE

Into the witness box, Constable, there'll be plenty of time for that later on.

The P.C. gets into the box, hitting at anyone within range.

PROSECUTION

You are P.C. Pan-Am?

POLICEMAN

No. I shall deny that to the last breath in my body.
(Prosecutor nods) Oh. Sorry, yes.

PROSECUTION

Do you recognize the defendant?

POLICEMAN

No. Never seen him before in my life. I swear it. Oh yes. He's the one. He done it all right. I'd recognize him anywhere, sorry sweetie.

PROSECUTION

Will you tell the court what happened?

POLICEMAN

Ho yus. I was proceeding in a northerly direction up Alitalia Street when I saw the deceased *(Pointing at defendant)* at an upstairs window, bearing her bosom at the general public. She then took off her…Wait a tick. That's the wrong story. Ho yus! There were three nuns on a train and the ticket inspector says to one of them *(Prosecutor shakes his head)*…No. Anyway, I clearly saw the deceased.

DEFENCE

Defendant.

POLICEMAN

Sorry. Sorry, sweetie. I clearly saw the defendant…doing whatever he's accused of. Red-handed. When kick…cautioned, he said "It's a fair cop, I did it all… Right, no doubt about that." Then, bound as he was to the chair, he assaulted me and three other offices while bouncing around the cell. The End.

Spontaneous applause from the court. Shouts of "More! More!" Pan-Am raises his hands and the clapping and shouting dies down.

POLICEMAN

Thank you! Thank you! And for my next piece of evidence I'd like to…

DEFENCE

That's enough thank you, Constable…

JUDGE

Excellent evidence, Constable…

Defence leaps up.

DEFENCE

Sir! I protest…I protest. *(Indicates Prosecuting Counsel)* He's had two goes, and I've only…

JUDGE

Shut up, I'm in charge of this court. *(To the court)* Stand up! *(Everyone stands up)* Sit down! *(Everyone sits down)* Go moo! *(Everyone goes moo)* Now order the unicyclist! *(Unicyclist comes in)* And on with the pixie hats! *(Everyone puts on pixie hats with large pointed ears)* And let's sing the silly song.

Everyone bursts into song:

COURTROOM

Anything goes in.
Anything goes out!
Fish, bananas, old pajamas,
Mutton! Beef! and trout!
Anything goes in!
Anything…

Finally and mercifully the sketch ends.

R.A.F. Banter

R.A.F. officer's mess.
Squadron Leader just back from a raid enters, taking off his flying helmet.

BOVRIL

Morning, Squadron Leader.

SQUAD

What ho, Squiffy.

BOVRIL

How was it?

SQUAD

Top hole. Bally Jerry pranged his kite right in the how's your father. Hairy blighter, dicky-birdied, feathered back on his Sammy, took a waspy, flipped over on his Betty Harper's and caught his can in the bertie.

BOVRIL

I don't think I quite follow you, Squadron Leader.

SQUAD

It's perfectly ordinary banter. *(Starting again – a touch slower and with hand movements)* Bally *Jerry*…pranged his kite right in the how's yer father… Hairy blighter…dicky-birdied, feathered back on his Sammy…took a waspy…flipped over on his Betty Harper's and caught his can in the bertie.

BOVRIL

No, I'm just not understanding banter at all well today, Squadron Leader. Give it to us slower.

SQUAD

Banter's not the same if you say it slower.

BOVRIL

Hold on. *(Calling across)* Wingo!

WINGO

Yes!

BOVRIL

Bend an ear to the Squadron Leader's banter for a sec. would you?

WINGO

Can do.

BOVRIL

Jolly good.

WINGO

Fire away.

SQUAD

(Draws a deep breath and looks slightly uncertain then starts even more deliberately than before)

Bally Jerry…pranged his kite, right in the how's yer father…Hairy blighter…dicky-birdied…feathered back on his Sammy…took a waspy…flipped over on his Betty Harper's…and caught his *can* in the *bertie*.

WINGO

No, I don't understand that banter at all.

SQUAD

Something up with my banter, chaps?

Siren goes. An out-of-breath Young Pilot rushes in holding his flying gear.

PILOT

Bunch of monkies on the ceiling, sir! Bag your egg and fours and let's get the bacon delivered.

General incomprehension. They look at each other.

WINGO

Do you understand that?

SQUAD

No, didn't understand a word of it.

WINGO

Sorry we don't understand.

PILOT

You know…bally ten-penny ones dropping in the custard… *(Searching for the words)*…er…oh…charlie choppers chucking a handful…

WINGO

No, no…sorry.

BOVRIL

Say it a bit slower.

PILOT

There's a sausage squad up the blue end.

SQUAD

No, still don't get it.

PILOT

Cabbage crates coming over the briny.

SQUAD

No.

Silly Election

Urgent documentary music.
Slides of Politicians in strange poses, intercut with Australian Animals.

Spot on desk stage left with lots of telephones on it.

At the desk, in suits, are:
Linkman, Norman, Gerald, and Colin

They have lots of papers on the desk, which they keep sorting through. From behind them.
Three very scantily-clad ladies keep appearing and bringing them fresh pieces of paper.

Music fades.
All at desk have hearing-aid-type earphones.

LINKMAN

Hello, and welcome to Election Night Special. There's great excitement here, as we should be getting the first result through any minute…we're not sure where it'll be from…it could be from Leicester or West Byfleet…the polling's been quite heavy in both areas…and wait a moment…I'm just getting a loud buzzing noise in my left ear. Excuse me. *(He bangs his ear and knocks a large bee out)* Eurrrrgghh! *(He swats it)* Let's go straight over to James Gilbert at Leicester.

Slides change to town hall exterior, with the caption "Leicester." F/X of a crowd's murmuring.

A Returning Officer stands in front of a group of half grey suited, half sillily dressed Candidates and Agents.
The silly ones in extraordinary hats, false noses, etc. The Returning Officer has a stand mike in front of him.

NORMAN

It's a straight fight in this seat here at Leicester… we're just about to hear the result. Behind the returning officer, you can see Arthur Smith the sensible candidate, and there is Jetheroe Walrustitty, the silly candidate, with his agent and his wife.

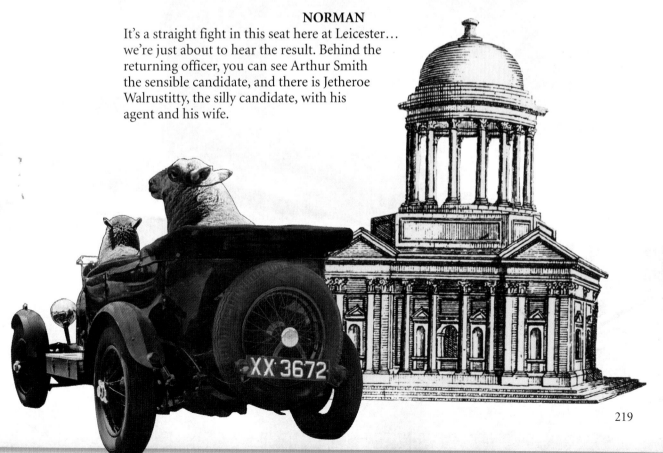

RETURNING OFFICER

Here is the result for Leicester. Arthur J. Smith…

VOICE-OVER

Sensible Party.

RETURNING OFFICER

30,612. Jetheroe Q. Walrustitty…

VOICE-OVER

Silly Party.

RETURNING OFFICER

32,108.

F/X of cheering from the crowd. Hand shaking, etc.

LINKMAN

Well, there's the first result and the Silly Party have held Leicester. Norman, what do you think about that?

NORMAN

It's more or less as I predicted, except that the Silly Party won. I think that this result is largely due to the number of votes cast. Gerald?

GERALD

Well, there's a swing here to the Silly Party…but how big a swing I'm not going to tell you.

NORMAN

I think one ought to point out that in this constituency, since the last election, a lot of very silly people have moved into a new housing estate and consequently a lot of sensible voters have moved further down the road, the other side of number 29.

LINKMAN

Well I can't add anything to that. Colin?

COLIN

Can I just say that this is the first time I've been on TV?

LINKMAN

No, no, we haven't time, because we're going straight over to Luton.

Mount Everest on slide with caption "Luton."

On stage a Returning Officer and Alan Jones, the Sensible candidate, K. Philips-Bong, and Tarquin.

MAN

Here at Luton, it's a three-cornered fight between Alan Jones, Sensible Party; Tarquin Fintimlinbinwhinbimlimbus-stop F'tang-F'tang-Ole-biscuitbarrel, Silly Party; and Keving Philips-Bong, who ran on the "Slightly Silly" ticket. And here's the result…

RETURNING OFFICER

Alan Jones…

VOICE-OVER

Sensible.

RETURNING OFFICER

9,112. Kevin Philips-Bong…

VOICE-OVER

Slightly Silly.

RETURNING OFFICER

Nought.
Tarquin Fintimlinbinwhinbimlimbus-stop F'tang-F'tang-Ole-biscuitbarrel…

VOICE-OVER

Silly.

RETURNING OFFICER

12,441.

VOICE-OVER

So the Silly Party have taken Luton.

LINKMAN

A gain for the Silly Party at Luton. The first gain of the Election – Norman?

NORMAN

This is a very significant result. A normally very sensible constituency
Luton, with a high proportion of people who aren't a bit silly, has gone
completely ga-ga.

LINKMAN

I've just heard that James Gilbert has with him the winning candidate
at Luton.

JAMES GILBERT

Tarquin, are you pleased with the result?

TARQUIN

Ho, jus! Me old beauty. I should say so. Baa, baa.

JAMES GILBERT

How do you see this result?

TARQUIN

(in high-pitched voice)

F'tang I see this as an overwhelming mandate to the Silly Party. *(He howls)*

LINKMAN

Do we have the swing at Luton?

GERALD

I've worked it out, but it's a secret.

LINKMAN

How about the swong?

NORMAN

I've got the swong here in this box, and it's looking fine. I can see through the breathing holes that it's eating peanuts up at a rate of knots.

LINKMAN

How about the swang?

GERALD

It's over 29 percent up above six hundred feet and slightly…

NORMAN

Can I break in here to say that the swing has just choked itself to death…it's lying in there with its little legs sticking in the air, and it fair turns your stomach.

COLIN

Can I just say this is the second time I've appeared on TV?

LINKMAN

Sorry, Sacha, we're just about to get another result.

Slide of Sydney Opera House, caption "Harpenden."

Another Returning Officer.

RETURNING OFFICER

Hullo, from Harpenden. We'll have the result in a moment. This is a significant seat because in addition to the official Silly candidate, there is an independent Very Silly candidate…

The Very Silly Candidate is in a large cube of polystyrene with prop legs sticking out, and one hand encased somewhere in the lump of concrete.

…who may split the Silly vote.

Mrs. Elsie Zzzzzzzzzzz…
(Obvious man in drag with enormous breasts)

VOICE-OVER

Silly.

RETURNING OFFICER

26,317. Jeanette Walker…

VOICE-OVER

Sensible.

RETURNING OFFICER

26,318.

VOICE-OVER

That was close.

RETURNING OFFICER

Malcolm Peter Brian Telescope Adrian Blackpool Rock Stoatgobbler John Raw Vegetable *(Sound of horse whinnying)* Norman Michael *(He rings a bell, he blows a whistle)* Smith *(Shot and he breaks glass)* Edwards *(Hoot and railway engine)* Thompson *(Moo)* *(He sings a snatch of "Well keep a welcome in the hillsides")* *(Three shots)* Williams *(Suwannee whistle)* *(Snatch of "Raindrops*

Keep Falling on My Head" and "Don't Sleep in the Subway, Darling") (Klaxon and elephant roar) Smith…

VOICE-OVER

Very Silly.

RETURNING OFFICER

2.

LINKMAN

Well, there you have it. A Sensible gain at Driffield with the Silly vote being split by Malcolm Peter Brian Telescope Adrian Blackpool Rock Stoatgobbler John Raw Vegetable *(Sound of horse whinnying)* Norman Michael *(He rings a bell, he blows a whistle)* Smith *(Shot and he breaks glass)* Edwards *(Hoot and railway engine)* Thompson *(Moo) (He sings a snatch of "Well keep a welcome on the hillside") (Three shots)* Williams *(Suwannee whistle) (Snatch of "Raindrops Keep Falling on My Head" and "Don't Sleep in the Subway, Darling") (Klaxon and elephant roar)* Smith…the Very Silly candidate.

And I've just heard that at Luton, Jimmy Gilbert has with him the unsuccessful Slightly Silly candidate, Kevin Philips-Bong.

Slide of Mount Everest with "Luton."

JAMES GILBERT

Kevin Philips-Bong. You polled no votes at all. Not a sausage. Are you disheartened?

BONG

Not at all. I regard this as a most encouraging result and as a massive vote of confidence in myself and my party.

Back to panel. Feverish activity, even greater air of dynamic urgency.

LINKMAN

A very brave Kevin Philips-Bong there – Norman.

NORMAN

Well, I've just heard from Luton that my auntie's ill – er – it's possibly gastroenteritis – Gerald.

GERALD

We've just had our front door painted.

LINKMAN

Could be…Norman.

NORMAN

It's certainly *faster,* but whether we can get more people in I don't know…

GERALD

Very wet indeed.

COLIN

Can I say that this is the last time I'm appearing on TV?

LINKMAN

No, I'm afraid you can't, we haven't got time. Just to bring you up to date with a few results you may have missed. A little pussy-cat has taken Barrow-in-Furness, that's a gain from the Liberals there. Simon Akwekwe has taken Enoch Powell's old seat – an important gain for Zambia there and…yes! Arthur Negus has held Bristols. That's not a result, that's just a piece of gossip…and Monsieur Pompidou has captured Oldham for the French Party, and two pieces of putty, a frog called "Kipper" and a mechanic from Dunbar have gone "Ni" in Blackpool. So it looks like a Silly landslide all over Britain – and with that prospect of five more silly years, it's goodbye from Election Night Special. We'll be back next week when we'll be talking about the economy with the Younger Generation and Fred Streeter.

Urgent music swells. Slides are changed more frenetically during this last speech.

Book Credits by Stanley Baldwin

Hello. Well, I was extremely pleased and honoured to be asked to write the credits for this book, not only because I believe that it is vital in this day and age for members of the older generation to keep pace with the dynamic and exciting ideas of youth, but also for the money.

Well, here goes – the splendid cast was headed by Richard Tauber and Edith Evans. I'm sorry…I lost my notes…ah, yes the book was written by John Cleese, Graham Chapman (I wonder if he's any relation to the Chapman I knew at Oxford who could gargle "Ave Maria" with a pint of claret)…er…Eric Idle, Terry Jones, Michael Palin (I wonder if he's any relation to the Chapman I knew at Cambridge who had a dancing parakeet who could sing "Rule Britannia" in Thai) with special star-guest award-winning artwork from the boisterous Terry Gilliam (who, I believe, is foreign-born though of course absolutely none the worse for it, and may well be related to the Chapman who worked for President Wilson at the Versailles Conference and who could fellate a fleetful of sailors during his morning break) where am I? Oh, yes…the very fine music was written and arranged by my old friend, oh there isn't any music it's a book, never mind, the cover of the book and all the artwork, including this little note of mine was designed and well…I'm not quite sure what the word is…laid out by Steve Kirwan with the help of another bottle of claret thank you, who is perhaps related to the Chapman who sold a regiment of Boers to the Nazis in exchange for another bottle of gin thank you…what? Sorry about that…I think I'll finish this in the morning.

Saturday morning.
The book was edited by Eric Idle and is none the worse for that. I've read many books far worse than this written by him so don't worry, Eric…er…now…where was I…oh yes…some very useful information here – the book was produced in the heart of Hollywood's sleazy NoHo area – where I believe you can now get an assisted massage and global rub for less than twelve dollars – and the publisher is none other than my old friend Willy Caldwell, who served with me in the Sudan – he had his leg shot off twice, and I'm very surprised to hear he's gone into book production. He was very ably assisted, not only by Betty McQueen Roper (no relation to the Roper of Roper's Glue) but also by seventeen stone eight pound Brian "The Thing" Campbell, both of whom went without the normal bodily functions for twenty-six days in order to prepare this reading experience…is that the hip phrase now?

Well, I think this is almost the end of my little piece. I'd like to say how much I've enjoyed writing it – hope I haven't left anyone out. I do go on a bit, I know – but I sincerely hope that you get as much pleasure from reading it as I have from not reading it…oh dear…that's not a very good way to end, is it?*

*No. [Ed.]

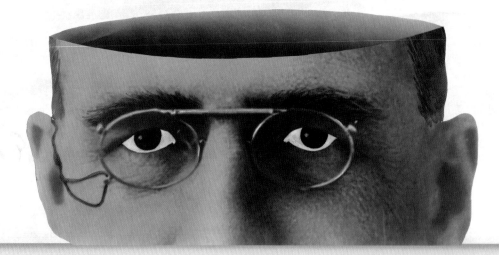

Monty Python would like to thank...

John Goldstone
Roger Saunders
Ian Miles
John Du Prez
Matt Bialer
Tom Hoberman
Nancy Lewis
Jim Beach
Anne James
Kath James
Alana Gospodnetich
Tony Smith
Harvey Goldsmith
David Sherlock
Steve Abbott
Hazel Pethig
Roger Last

Tim Brooke-Taylor
for permission to reprint *The Four Yorkshiremen*
(co-written with Marty Feldman and John Cleese)

Pantheon Books for permission to reprint many sketches
from *Monty Python's All the Words, Volumes 1 and 2*

Methuen Books for permission to reprint excerpts from
Graham Chapman's *A Liar's Autobiography*

Michael Palin for permission to reprint
excerpts from his diaries

Spot the Difference

Both these and the next pages are identical, yet they have seven slight changes. See if you can spot the differences.

Spot the Difference (cont.)

Spot the differences between these and the previous pages. You can WIN a Weekend for Two with Hugh Jackman or a chance to own the underwear of one of the Pythons.

Eat More Pork

At Booksellers Near You!

The Wife of Brian
by Monty Python

A penetrating look at the little-known woman behind it all.

Price: $16.95

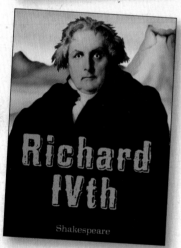

Shakespeare's Richard IVth

A play about Dick Cheney. A study in evil. Monty Shakespeare's dark tragedy about a man who chose himself to lead from behind.

Price: $18.95

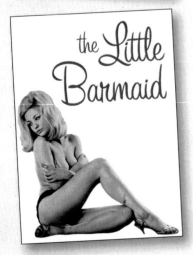

The Little Barmaid

The perennial classic. A delight for dipsomaniac children everywhere.

Price: $14.95